# You CAN Get There From Here

Bruce
Thank you!
Love Me!

Dear Reader,
Thank you!
Love Mel

# You CAN Get There From Here

An Easy-to-Follow
Guide for Using
the Law of Attraction,
Tapping (EFT & MTT), and
Visualization to Take You
from Where You Are Now to the
Life of Your Dreams

Melinda Weese Anderson

Copyright © 2010 MELINDA WEESE ANDERSON

All rights reserved. No portion of this book may be reproduced mechanically, electronically, or by any other means, including photocopying, without written permission of the publisher. It is illegal to copy this book, post it to a website, or distribute it by any other means without permission from the publisher.

Melinda Weese Anderson
Live In The Moment
10053 – 1145 Innisfil Beach Road
Innisfil, Ontario, Canada L9S 4Y7
Mel.LiveInTheMoment@rogers.com
www.liveinthemoment.ca

Limits of Liability and Disclaimer of Warranty
The author and publisher shall not be liable for your misuse of this material. This book is strictly for informational and educational purposes.

Warning – Disclaimer
The purpose of this book is to educate and entertain. It is not intended to replace a one-on-one relationship with a qualified health care professional and is *definitely not* intended as medical advice, diagnosis, or treatment. If you are under the care of any health professionals (or should be), the author and/or publisher strongly encourage you to discuss any and all modifications in your diet, lifestyle, exercise program, nutrition, or the use of EFT or MTT with them prior to making any changes, and never discontinue or reduce prescription medications without consulting your doctor or pharmacist.

By practicing the techniques in this book, please be aware that you will very likely experience emotions and in so doing you take full responsibility for your own well-being.

The author and/or publisher does not guarantee that anyone following these techniques, suggestions, tips, ideas, or strategies will become successful. The author and/or publisher shall have neither liability nor responsibility to anyone with respect to any loss or damage caused, or alleged to be caused, directly or indirectly by the information contained in this book.

ISBN: 978-0-9865822-0-2

# What Clients Are Saying About Working with Mel

(names have been withheld to honor client confidentiality)

*"I have been a participant and a presenter at many workshops over the years and I would honestly say this workshop was the best I have ever attended."*

*"I will say I thought this was going to be a waste of time and only went because I was forced to by a friend. I am now sold 100% on the techniques I learned today. I was extremely impressed by how quickly they worked and Mel was amazing!"*

*"I never dreamt that this short workshop would be so powerful and enlightening."*

*"This course opened my eyes to a therapeutic technique I've never been exposed to before. It was very interesting and best of all IT WORKS. Mel is very passionate and compassionate about teaching others."*

*"I didn't think this was going to help me. However, my mind has been changed!"*

*"Mel, you are magical with EFT!"*

*"Mel is a supportive, motivating and most importantly a down to earth presenter. It is great to participate in a workshop where the proof is in the experience, not in the presenter's ability to 'sell' the technique."*

*"Thanks so much for the session yesterday. I felt totally at ease with you and felt like you were truly connected and most of all so professional as well as caring. I have done EFT before but never ever felt anything like I did yesterday. I also liked the way you thoroughly explained everything making sure I understood the hows and whys. I am so inspired to keep going! Thank you so much Mel!"*

## And just two of the testimonials from the pilot program participants of Mel's soon-to-be-available 12-week weight-loss support program, "The Last (or First) 20 Lbs."

*"When I started this program, I thought it was just about losing weight. After the first night I realized it was so much more. It's about how we feel about ourselves. How we can empower ourselves. How ONLY WE can change how we feel."*

*"I signed up because it sounded like a weight loss program and I've never been able to overcome my addiction to food.... I am so pleased that in addition to losing weight, Mel was able to help me break through and rise above a very difficult personal loss in my life (my Dad's passing). I have never felt more at peace or more OK with that loss than I do right now."* (Two months after the program, this participant wrote to say that, by combining her own efforts with what she'd experienced in the program, she's lost over 20 pounds and 18.5 inches!)

*To my darling Angel son, Tyler.
My greatest inspiration and joy.
And my greatest teacher.*

*To Dr. Wayne Dyer.
Your words of wisdom have carried me
from the depth of my
darkness to a world of light I previously
couldn't have imagined existed.*

*To Gary Craig.
You are a gift to humanity.
My profound gratitude to you for
creating and sharing
EFT with the world.*

# Acknowledgments

My heartfelt gratitude to the many people who have impacted my life and supported me on my journey. In no particular order my deepest gratitude and appreciation goes out to: My darling Tyler of course, my inspiration, my love, my little Angel. You've given my life deeper purpose and meaning than I thought possible, and every day you further inspire me to do this work so the world you grow into is a more loving world. My hope is that I evolve as fast as you need me to! To my ex-husband, Kim, thank you for the love we shared. However brief, it was so meaningful as we brought Tyler into the world! I wish you all the love and happiness imaginable.

To Jilly, John, and the kids: thanks for always being there. And also to Jilly, although we see the world rather differently, I so appreciate your constant love and non-judgmental support. La you! To Roger and Jazz, you've been there supporting me though the ups and downs over the past 10 years: through the March Mutiny, my father's death, my re-location, my marriage, two miscarriages, the birth of my son, the end of my marriage, and my mom's death, quite a journey and I'm so appreciative of all the support, the humor, and the hugs. To my pals at the Bradford Toastmasters, thank you for helping me find my voice and lose my shaky hands. To Cynthia Barlow at Constellation Learning, thank you for your loving support during Life Skills, the Trust Program, and beyond; such an amazing and powerful start to my healing journey. To Timo, thank you for teaching me the value of AFGOs; a whole new way to look at things! To my Mastermind pals: Jennifer Allen-Green, Jamie Broughton, Gillian Todd-Messinger, Steve Marsh, and Derek MacNeil, you guys rock! Thank you so much for the "tough love." Because of your unwavering loving support, I was inspired to define and step into a totally phenomenal life! And to all my wonderful friends and colleagues who've shown up at the most perfect time, you are so amazing and I love you!

To Dr. Wayne Dyer, while you're completely unaware of this, from the first book of yours I read years ago while I was still in the dark and struggling, to the books and audio programs I continue to read and listen to today, I feel like I'm your long-distance ninth child. I grew up with you but, more importantly, I woke up, so to speak, because of you. To Gary Craig, every day I am in appreciation to you for this amazing gift you gave to the world. I would not be living my life with such joy today were it not for you. To Louise Hay, the first time I read your book *You Can Heal Your Life*, I so wasn't ready for it. Since then I've read it numerous times, and each time I get something more. Thank you for the inspiration and the vast array of information you provide.

A huge thank you to all the wonderful EFT and MTT Practitioners and Masters who offer a multitude of amazing products and training materials. To Paul Widdershoven of School Made Much Easier and Life Made Much Easier, thank you for supporting me in stepping into myself as a "Zig-er" even when everyone else in my world at the time was zagging." Those early days of "zigging" became much easier with your support! To Till Schilling and TappyBear, you rock! And I still maintain that every child, and bigger kids up to at least age 55–60 or so, would benefit from welcoming a TappyBear into their home.

To the various Law of Attraction teachers I've learned so much from: Ester and Jerry Hicks with the teachings of Abraham, Bob Doyle of Wealth Beyond Reason, Mike Dooley of TUT.com, and Michael Losier of LawOfAttractionBook.com right here in Canada, thank you all so much. To my favorite "Belief Guys," Gregg Braden and Bruce Lipton, you both put words, definition, and clarity to some of the abstract thoughts and inklings I've held but couldn't fully articulate. It all makes so much sense when you say it! To Joe Vitale: from Buying Trances to Hypnotic Writing tips to Ho'oponopono with Dr. Hew Len, you rock and, I love you, I'm sorry, please forgive me, thank you! To my favorite Mentor Coach Christian Mickelsen from CoachesWithClients. com, who not only has great training programs but has a plethora of awesome resources. To my book-writing mentor, Donna Kozik from MyBigBusinesscard.com, who has *the* book-writing formula! And this book is the proof of that.

And last, but certainly not least, to all my clients and workshop participants who have honored me with their trust and allowed me to take part in their healing journey. My life is richer because each of you has taken part in it.

Love and Light to you all.

# About the Author

Melinda Weese Anderson (Mel for short) is an EFT and MTT Practitioner and Transformation Coach specializing in the Law of Attraction and Visualization. Mel is the founder of Live In The Moment, a company dedicated to empowering individuals to step into the life of their dreams—their Phenomenal Life, regardless of the starting point they're currently at.

After many years of reliving the traumas and dramas of an abusive childhood and painful past (which robbed her of any hope for a happy future) Mel went on a quest for a happier way to live.

Guided by an inner voice that unwaveringly declared "I can choose happiness," Mel found her way.

And now through Live In The Moment, Mel partners with individuals to guide them on their way. Through private and group EFT/MTT sessions, workshops, retreats, and Transformation Coaching programs, Mel shares the very tools she learned and used.

No matter where you're starting from, if you're ready to choose happiness for your life, using the tools that Mel shares is a powerful step in the right direction.

# Contents

| | | |
|---|---|---:|
| Introduction | | 17 |
| **Part I:** | **You Are Here: Up Until Now, Deciding, and Stepping Out of It** | **19** |
| Chapter 1: | Failure Isn't an Option, but Survival Isn't Enough | 21 |
| Chapter 2: | It's All an Inside Job! | 29 |
| Chapter 3: | The Meaning of Life | 35 |
| **Part II:** | **The Bridge: Tools to Get You to Your Destination** | **57** |
| Chapter 4: | The Law of Attraction as Child's Play | 59 |
| Chapter 5: | Tapping: EFT & MTT; A Funny Thing Happened | 73 |
| Chapter 6: | Visualization…With a Twist! | 105 |
| **Part III:** | **Your Destination—Your Phenomenal Life: "From Now Often," Choosing, and Stepping Into It** | **119** |
| Chapter 7: | Never Mind! | 121 |
| Chapter 8: | Hold the Pickles | 129 |
| Chapter 9: | Keep Your Eye on the Prize | 139 |

# Introduction

Have you ever known someone who, despite their best intentions and efforts, seems to be stuck in a life that really isn't all they've dreamt of? It's good and they experience great times…but something isn't quite right.

Perhaps you've heard them talk about how they've tried to improve things with systems, programs, or books. And you've even seen them taking all the "right steps" to move things forward, but nothing seems to stick.

Day in and day out, there's always this feeling that something bigger or brighter is eluding them. They have a perpetual feeling of "there's got to be more to life than this." They may get close to their dreams, and then things just seem to slip slowly back into the regular routine. Or worse, they achieve what they're striving for but, the moment they do, almost instantly, something bigger and "badder" comes along that totally wipes out the joy of their accomplishment.

Or, maybe you've known someone who has simply resigned to the fact that joy and happiness are for other people, and regular folks like themselves need to just knuckle down and settle in to what they have, and stop all this "whimsical fantasy-life" nonsense.

Perhaps Mondays are dreaded and Fridays are a cause for celebration. And every day in between Monday and Friday is just a countdown. Same-ol', same-ol'—day after day and week after week.

But still, somewhere, deep down, is an undeniable yearning for more.

If this sounds a bit like you or someone you know, this fun and fast-paced read is the jump-start and road map you've been looking for. In the pages that follow, I show you how to see what's blocking you and keeping you stuck, what to do about it, and how to move beyond it without sliding back afterward.

The ideas and tools I share with you are down to earth, and they're easy to understand and incorporate into your life. And they've even been fully tested "in the field." That test field is my own life, so I know they work!

As you start the book you might feel a bit like you do when you start watching a movie and you don't quite get the early scenes. But when you stay with the movie as the plot unfolds, by the end you're going, "Oh, I get it now.... In the beginning when they did that...and then that other thing.... Oh, it all goes together now.... Cool!" That's a bit like how this book is put together for you.

In the first section things might seem a little like those early scenes in the movie. Then the second section is a bit like the plot developing, and by the third section, I'll tie it all in together and wrap it all up so everything from the first two sections will become very clear.

So, if you're ready to give up being stuck and wanting more out of life, I invite you to read on to discover how.

# I

# You Are Here: Up Until Now, Deciding, and Stepping Out of It

*The wake doesn't steer the boat.*
~ Dr. Wayne Dyer

# Chapter 1

## Failure Isn't an Option, but Survival Isn't Enough

# Failure Isn't an Option, but Survival Isn't Enough

Once upon a time there was a young girl who, at the age of 4, moved with her mother and sister into a small apartment (but it was still big enough for her to do cartwheels clear across the living room before the furniture arrived, much to the dismay of her mom). She was told that her mom and dad had "separated" and this was the place she would now call home.

One wonderful memory of those days came about a few years later when the swimming pool was built in the park up the hill.

This was her favorite place to be. Something about the water made her feel truly alive. She practiced and practiced so she could pass the test and be granted entry into the deep end. She even volunteered to be the one to clean the dirty mark at the water's edge before the pool opened each day just so she could get in the pool as early as possible in the morning. Such fond memories of those long summer days of practically living in the water she loved so much.

Sadly, aside from the bright sunshine and fun in the water, her life was another story altogether.

You see, this little girl also came to the conclusion, at a very young age, that life was mostly a dark and painful place. Her childhood was filled with the physical and emotional pain of sexual abuse, and she was sworn to keep secrets that no child should ever have to keep.

As the years passed, her feelings of being very different and alone grew in proportion to her years. And even when the majority of the abuse ended after ten long years, the pain and insecurity of living with an alcoholic mother escalated and took its place.

At the age of 18 she left home and school, and entered into the workforce.

Work became a place to hide and bury her emptiness by being busy. But somehow, the feelings of worthlessness and self-loathing surfaced time and again, so she turned to "partying" to escape the emptiness of her dreary existence.

For close to the next two decades she oscillated between excessive drinking and various other self-destructive activities in an attempt to numb the pain, to progressing at work and consuming everything she possibly could from the "self-help" sections of the bookstores to overcome the pain.

It was a life of one step forward and two steps back.

Then one morning, rather than waking with the usual hangover, exhaustion, and dread of yet another day, something completely different happened.

On that particular morning, a very unfamiliar feeling was present when she opened her eyes and shook off the haziness of sleep. Strangely, it was a feeling of optimism.

The optimism was accompanied by a most unusual thought—a thought that was as clear as any thought could ever be, so clear it was actually a "knowing" more than just a thought.

On that morning she woke with a feeling of optimism and a "knowing" that she could choose happiness!

It was so clear to her that she knew she could never *not* know it again! Nothing had changed, and yet everything had changed. And it was on that morning, with that optimism and that "knowing," that she started living her life rather than living as if life was happening to her.

That morning was in September 2000, and the girl in the story is me.

From all that I've experienced, I know what it feels like to feel overwhelmed, hopeless, and alone, and to consider suicide as a possible solution. I know what if feels like to believe life is happening to me and that I should just settle with the lousy hand I've been dealt. I know what it feels like to believe that happiness and joy are for other people and that my lot in life is about just getting through it unless I end it.

And I know that, by making a choice, it can all be turned around.

I now believe that in each moment we have the opportunity to choose our reaction to everything going on around us. And our lives become the result of the choices we make. And when it happens that our choices take us somewhere we don't want to be, then it's up to us to choose again. It's always up to us, and it's only up to us.

> *My will shall shape the future. Whether I fail or succeed will be no man's doing but my own. I am the force; I can clear any obstacle before me or I can be lost in the maze. My choice; my responsibility; win or lose, only I hold the key to my destiny.*
>
> ~ Elaine Maxwell

## Be Where You Are

We all have a story that has been the truth of our life up until now. And whether your story is dark and traumatic or much lighter but you're at an equally unsatisfying point in your life now, the key to moving beyond it is to identify and accept that you are where you are right now.

Be it good, bad, or indifferent, identifying your true feelings (the ones you feel when you're not putting on a brave face for the benefit of others) about being where you are now is the first step to making peace with your life's story.

To get you started in this direction, please complete the Success and Happiness Rating exercise that follows. You might also want to have a journal handy from here onward, as there will be lots of opportunities for you to "capture your thoughts" by writing them in your journal as you're reading.

For the various areas of life, rate your feelings of success and/or happiness on a scale of 1 to 10 (1 = feeling very unsuccessful or very unhappy and 10 = feeling very successful or very happy).

Then use the space provided to jot a few notes about why your rating is what it is.

1. Work/Career: Rating 1-10 _____ and why

_____

_____

_____

_____

_____

# You CAN Get There From Here

2. Finances: Rating 1-10 _____ and why

   _____

   _____

   _____

   _____

3. Environments (home, work, etc.): Rating 1-10 _____ and why

   _____

   _____

   _____

   _____

4. Health/Wellness/Spirit: Rating 1-10 _____ and why

   _____

   _____

   _____

   _____

5. Personal/Professional Growth: Rating 1-10 _____ and why

_____

_____

_____

_____

_____


6. Personal Relationships with Partner and/or Children:
   Rating 1-10 _____ and why

_____

_____

_____

_____


7. Family (parents and siblings) and Friends:
   Rating 1-10 _____ and why

_____

_____

_____

_____

_____

8. Fun and Recreation: Rating 1-10 _____ and why

_____

_____

_____

_____

_____

We'll refer to this exercise a bit later, but for now, if you were a little surprised with anything you noted, feel free to do some additional journaling on the thoughts and feelings that came up for you in completing this exercise.

# Chapter 2

## It's All an Inside Job!

## It's All an Inside Job!

Imagine yourself sitting high atop a mighty, powerful elephant. You're prepared for this. You've taken the training courses, read the books, and watched all the available DVDs on elephant training.

Today is your day! The time has come when *you* are going to have the elephant follow your commands so you will be certified as an elephant trainer.

Your elephant trainer examiner gives you the nod, and you begin the test. Your first task is to lead the mighty elephant to a target off to your left. So you give the elephant the "start now" nudge with your left foot. And—ta-da—like magic, the mighty animal moves to the left. A feeling of elation and pride washes over you, and you feel your smile emerging as you continue with confidence.

But then—wait a minute. What's happening? Your thoughts race in horror as you feel the mighty animal stop, then take an even more powerful stomp to the right...and then another...and another. *"No,"* you think. "This can't be!"

Immediately your thoughts go to your training. You've learned what to do in this situation. You execute the "regaining control" strategy maneuver you learned and practiced so many times—and it works! The motion to the right stops. You breathe a sigh of relief, feeling elated and somewhat lucky. Then you employ more of the strategies you've learned, and the mighty elephant moves slowly to the left again.

But horror or horrors, he stops and turns right again. So you employ more of what you've learned. You analyze the situation, throw in some logic, and even try to reason with him. He's still not moving to the left. You try willpower and all the brute strength you can muster...and... nothing, other than another blasted stomp to the right!

Things are not looking good right now, and you notice the examiner is looking down at the ground shaking his head. The test is over, and today you are not certified.

You just don't understand. You've done everything the training taught you to do, and the elephant continues to do what he wants.

As the other trainer comes to guide you and the mighty elephant back in, you exchange words and he offers some encouragement. You both agree that "it just wasn't meant to be" and you step down from your mount.

While this is obviously a fictitious story, it illustrates what goes on for many of us on a regular basis as we try to make changes in our lives. We read books and take courses, and, when we feel we're ready, we launch ourselves out there to make the changes. Things seem great when "it's working," but when it's not, it's a totally different story.

This problem of it "not working" comes about because usually we don't give any consideration to what's going on within us. We look outside of ourselves and attempt to control or change our environment to produce the feelings of success or happiness we're looking to experience on the inside.

The flaw with this is that attempting to create pleasant feelings inside of ourselves by trying to control our environment is about as effective as attempting to fix our hair by reaching up to comb the hair of our reflection in the mirror. It just doesn't work that way!

## Inside-Out vs. Outside-In

These days, more than ever, we humans seem to be caught up in an outside-in trap. We're constantly looking for people, places, and things outside of us to alter what we feel on the inside, when really, the only way to enjoy the people, places, and things outside of ourselves is to work from the inside-out.

Going back to the elephant story, let's say that the mighty elephant in that story represents your subconscious mind—that 95 some-odd percent of the mind that we don't have access to. And you, as the rider on top, represent the 5 or so percent of your mind (your conscious mind) that you do have access to. This would be your thoughts and memories.

As illustrated in the story, the mighty elephant is going to do pretty much whatever he darn well pleases regardless of what you have to say about it because, based on size alone, you are simply no match for him, and he knows that.

This is somewhat how it is with our subconscious and conscious minds: The subconscious is much bigger and our smaller conscious mind is no match.

What does this have to do with living the life of your dreams? Well, most of us come at change with our conscious mind leading the way.

Just like the elephant rider in our story. We prepare ourselves and, when we *think* we're ready, we tackle something new. And the results aren't always what we've hoped for.

So what happens? To explain this even further, a very brief overview of the subconscious mind (and I mean *very* brief) is that every experience you've ever had from, say, the time of birth until now is stored in your subconscious mind. *Every single experience—ever!*

That's a lot of data you've got stored in there. Out of all of it, even with the very best recall, you can only get at about 5 percent of it.

What this means is that all kinds of stuff you have absolutely no recollection of whatsoever is still in there, actively running the show. Because, oh yes, the other really important thing about your subconscious mind is that one of its main, as in primary, as in before anything else, jobs, is to keep you safe.

So to keep you safe, the subconscious filters every thought, feeling, and action you have or take through this vast database of stored memories, and it basically has two sides that everything gets slotted into: This is good—do more; or, this is *not* good—stop immediately and never do this again!

There's not much gray area there. It's either good = do more, or bad = stop immediately.

One more thing: The criteria for filtering things into the "keeping you safe—good or bad" categories that your subconscious runs *everything* through were completed, closed, and set in place by the time you were about 7 years old. So everything you're experiencing today is being run through a "keeping you safe—good or bad" filtration system based on what would keep you safe up to the age of 7.

Is it just me, or are you getting the picture of how this might not be working so well for us—particularly when we try to make changes or move ourselves forward in life as adults?

Unless we find some way to get into that file system to update it, we could be trapped by our subconscious for a very long time. And, millions of people around the world who are struggling and feeling like they can't move forward in life are indeed trapped unknowingly by their subconscious. But you're not one of them!

# Decide!

You are about to embark on quite an adventure. You might want to think of the rest of this book as a "change room" of sorts.

There will be times when I'm sharing some really "out there" kind of strange stuff. As Dr. Wayne Dyer says in many of his seminars, "I'm telling you it's possibly even 'woo woo' and esoteric in advance so that you don't think that I don't know."

Because it kind of is "woo woo," and I know it! And you may just think so, too. But, if you hang with me until the end and even try the exercises along the way, I'm pretty certain you'll be glad you did, despite the "woo-ness" of it all.

So consider it a change room where I'm offering a bunch of ideas, tools, and different perspectives for you to try on. And in this change room, you can try them and decide what you like, what fits, and what's maybe not for you at this time.

I once heard it said that all words ending in "-cide" were about killing something. Now I'm no word-whiz, but from the few "-cide" words that immediately leapt into my thoughts (suicide, pesticide, and homicide) the rule seemed to hold true.

By deciding that your life is worth spending an hour or two reading and by further deciding that you're worth it by incorporating some potentially zany tools into your life to try them on, you're going to be "killing off" all the reasons, excuses, and justifications you've been holding for not stepping into the life of your dreams. So dare to take a stand for your life and decide now!

> *Decision is a risk rooted in the courage of being free.*
>
> ~ Paul Tillich

# Chapter 3

## The Meaning of Life

I suspect you probably didn't expect I'd jump right in with a topic this big so early in the book, but I wanted to get this right out there in the open.

So here goes: The meaning of life is…life is meaningless!

Now wait, I can understand that this is a bold statement, and I certainly don't mean it in an "it's all pointless, so go crazy then give up" sort of way. Not at all, and quite the contrary.

I mean it in the most empowering way imaginable.

You see, life, in and of itself, doesn't have meaning. Nothing is inherently good or bad in life. We get to make life mean whatever we choose. Every year, every day, every event, and every interaction—everything! It's all up to us; we get to apply the meaning to everything.

For example, if it's raining out, what does it mean? To the farmer who's been experiencing a drought it's wonderful; it means there's hope for his crops. To the family who's just started a short but long-awaited "fun in the sun" vacation, it's bad—at least one day of their very short vacation is ruined.

So just in this case alone, rain can be both good and bad, and can offer hope and be equated with sadness. But the point is that the meaning is completely dependent upon the people experiencing the events.

I understand that you may leap to a global perspective and challenge me on this regarding some of the world events that are going on and, while that would definitely be an interesting conversation (and one I've had numerous times with workshop participants), for the intent of this book, I'd like you to bring in your focus to only take in your own life.

As in, the relevance of this to you in your life is that you get to apply the meanings to every happening in your life. So there you are, going about your day-to-day existence and, without even knowing you're doing it, you're freely assigning meanings to the various occurrences and making your life mean whatever you say. This meaning designation is even more interesting because there are no "meaning police" dropping in randomly to check on you and the meanings you're coming up with. So once you assign something a meaning, it's pretty much a given that that's exactly what it means, unless you change it.

I caught myself in this meaning-assignment act not so long ago.

It was when I was still struggling to take off some weight. I had chosen to wear a comfy, cargo-style skirt and put it on. It seemed a bit looser, and that brought a smile to my lips. But nothing could have prepared me for what happened next. As I slid my favorite belt through the last loop and went to do it up, holy cow—it buckled two full holes over from where I usually wore it.

I was elated! I did a very brief Happy Dance right there and then double-checked and, sure enough, it was true. My belt was comfortably sitting two full holes tighter on me than I traditionally wore it. I had lost weight!

Well, *this* was incredible, to say the least! I had wanted to lose weight but was not really doing much about it. But that day, boy was I a healthy eater.

That day it didn't even enter my thoughts to reach for anything "sinful" in the food department. The foods I consumed that day were the healthiest I had in the house, and they even tasted better than normal. I made certain I drank lots of water, and the whole day was punctuated with my belief that I had somehow lost weight and I was certainly going to continue on that momentum now that I was aware of it.

Well, my little spontaneous weight-loss bubble was burst the next day when I pulled on a pair of slacks and again paired them with my favorite belt. As I did up the belt, the "two holes over" hole that I so joyously used the day before was sitting right where it usually did: two holes over from where I fastened my belt.

What??!!! How could this be? I had lost weight! I ate healthy all day! How did I gain "two belt holes' worth of weight" back overnight? I looked to my reflection in my mirror and I looked the same as the day before. But there, looking back at me, was the answer.

That comfy cargo skirt from the day before sat much higher, and the belt rested up closer to my waist. The slacks I was wearing that day perched somewhat lower, and the "waist band" was closer to hip level.

Ugh! I hadn't lost weight; I had simply worn my belt closer to my waist (which is considerably narrower than my hips).

In that instant I was both disappointed and enlightened. Disappointed for obvious reasons as anyone who has tried to lose weight understands. Seeing that first glimpse of success is nothing short of euphoria, so to have held it in my hands and lost it the next day was a letdown of monumental proportions.

*But*, I was also enlightened. The day before, I assigned a meaning to the belt holes that totally empowered me. And no one stepped in to tell me I was wrong because this whole meaning-labeling was done in my thoughts. For the whole day, my every action, how I ate, and even my posture (aka standing tall and proud like a peacock) were affected by the meaning I assigned in my own thoughts.

That day, based on the meaning I assigned to how my belt buckled, my beliefs, my feelings, my thoughts, and my actions were all affected by a meaning that I had assigned to something as minute as how my belt bucked up.

Very interesting stuff, this idea that one can assign any meaning they choose to the situations in their life, don't you think?

> *In the book of life, the answers aren't in the back.*
>
> ~ Charlie Brown

Take a moment to jot some notes (in the space provided or in your journal) about the main events that have shaped your life so far, and also begin to identify what meanings you've applied to these situations.

Between ages 1 and 10

_____

_____

_____

_____

_____

Between ages 11 and 20

_____

_____

_____

_____

_____

Between ages 21 and 30

_____

_____

_____

_____

_____

Between ages 31 and 40

_____

_____

_____

_____

_____

Between ages 41 and 50

From age 51 onward

Describe any patterns you noticed from doing this exercise.

After reflecting about this, if your life were a movie, what would the main plot and sub-plots be? What type of movie is it? Use the space below to briefly describe your life movie.

_____

_____

_____

_____

_____

_____

_____

_____

_____

_____

## Beliefs

> *Whether you believe you can or you can't, you're right!*
>
> ~ Henry Ford

This idea of the meanings we assign to the things in our life stems from something a little deeper—and that is our beliefs.

There is lots of great information on this topic, and it is one I'm totally fascinated by and have done a fair bit of looking into lately. But, once again, in the interest of taking a very big topic and chunking it down to what I consider the barest of essentials, I'm going to give you my bare-bones, no-fluff version of how our beliefs affect our life.

First, my definition of belief in this context is that a belief is a thought, view, or conviction you have about how the world works. It is your rules for what is true or right about how your life is going to work out based on your life experiences. Our individual beliefs are just that: individual. Each person's beliefs are as unique to them as their appearance.

So where do these unique-to-each-of-us beliefs come from, you might wonder. Well, from the time we're born (and some say it's even pre-birth, but, for simplicity here, I'll focus from birth onward) we begin soaking up all the energy, moods, words, and happenings going on around us and storing them in our subconscious mind.

And we're soaking in everything—every experience and feeling we have and observe. All of these things we're taking in are coming mostly from the people closest to us, who usually have the best intentions (but sometimes not). These folks are our parents, grandparents, siblings, friends, teachers, coaches, religious leaders we see, and people in authority like police, etc.

We're like little belief sponges soaking up everything we encounter from all the people, places, and experiences we encounter during our early childhood years up until the age of 7 (there's that magical age again, just as I mentioned about the subconscious before). All of this data we take in is the earliest data that gets stored in our subconscious, and in addition to becoming the "this is good—do more" *or* "this is bad—stop immediately" sorting data I mentioned earlier, it also becomes the basis of our belief system.

Also like the data-sorting system, the beliefs system is also pretty much complete by the age 7. By then we've formed the basics of our beliefs, and this becomes our internal code for how life works our individual set of rules. From then on, we live the rest of our lives by these beliefs, and they become a bit of a self-fulfilling prophecy.

Everything you see and experience gets filtered through your beliefs and perceived in a way that fits with those beliefs. This, in turn, validates and reinforces the truth of the beliefs for us.

This is a great system when we're considering things that are empowering and propelling us forward with inspiration. (Think of my temporary belief about my two-holes-over belt buckling story that inspired me to joyfully take appropriate action with regard to losing weight.) However, this whole beliefs filter can be problematic when the beliefs we hold aren't empowering, or, worse, if they're limiting and keeping us from accomplishing that which we want.

For example, the moment I realized my mistake with the belt, I vaguely remember also thinking things like: "Who was I kidding? Losing weight is way harder than that." "I'll never lose weight. I'm the chubby daughter, remember?" and "I'm the smart one and my sister is slim." This barrage of nasty thoughts continued on and on.

These not-so-pleasant "voices in my head" were telling me my true beliefs. The things I had internalized and made my rules for living. The things I heard growing up and then found life evidence to support and reinforce. And once grown, they've been the very things I then told myself over and over—especially each and every time I attempted to lose weight.

These are called "limiting beliefs." They're limiting because they limit us from moving beyond them. Day in and day out, you live your life according to your beliefs, no matter what, even if doing so is in opposition to what you say you want.

Given that most of your beliefs are formed by the time you're 7 years of age, and they are also stored in the subconscious (whose primary role is to keep you safe) one could argue that all beliefs you hold are limiting you to some degree. I won't delve into that discussion here, but it certainly is an interesting item to ponder.

Here's another example of how this plays out in our lives. Suppose you're currently struggling at work and, despite changing jobs a few times, you always seem to end up feeling like it's a struggle.

Chances are that, at some point in your early development, you adopted a belief such as "life is hard" or "no pain no gain." Maybe you heard this at home from your parents about working. Or maybe you heard it from a coach about winning the game. Or from any number of well-intentioned sources who were trying to encourage to you to persevere when the going got tough. But now, it's serving more as a limitation as you continue to experience the "pain," believing it's part of the "gain."

Or maybe you want to experience financial abundance, but can't seem to get beyond living paycheck to paycheck. It could be that at some point you adopted a negative view of wealthy people. Maybe you soaked up "rich people are mean," "rich people are greedy," or even "rich people are all crooks." If any of these formulated your beliefs, you will do everything in your power to not be wealthy because, if you dared to be wealthy, it would mean you were one of those "mean, greedy, crooked" rich people. So you see, no matter what you say and no matter what action you take, you will continue to be not wealthy because you must adhere to your beliefs.

At this point I like to say that, just like the weather in my rainy-day example earlier, beliefs in and of themselves aren't good or bad. They simply "are," and they are in place to keep us safe. But, if you're feeling about as deflated as I did upon discovering my error with my belt, take heart: There is a bright side to all of this. You see now that you're aware of this, and because earlier you decided to take a stand for your life and try on something different, now you get to do just that.

Because although it appears our beliefs are cemented in to our subconscious forever, with the tools I'll be sharing with you shortly, that doesn't have to be how it is.

But, in order to move forward with our beliefs, we first need to figure out what they are. Given most are in that 95 percent subconscious we don't have access to, we can't just list them and get to work. (For some that you do know, this will work, and I encourage you to jot these down.) For the ones you can't just rhyme off, I have a couple of ways to go about bringing them to the surface to start to identify them.

To get started, choose an area of your life that you're trying to make changes in but, up until now, you've not had success with. If you don't quite know what to focus on, have a look at your Happy/Success ratings from earlier. Is there an area that's rated low that you've been attempting to make changes in? If so, try this exercise in that area.

With your area of focus in mind, think back to your childhood and list some of the influential people in your life at that time (e.g., mother, father, teacher, aunts, uncles, grandparents, etc.).

_____

_____

_____

_____

_____

Next, list any of the "family stories" or "rules" you remember these people saying and what they meant (e.g., Nanna always said that children should be seen and not heard, meaning that I needed to keep quiet, especially around people of authority).

_____

_____

_____

_____

_____

_____

Now, with the examples above, list some of the evidence in your life now that's been reinforcing this for you (e.g., To this day I never speak up to my boss or any authority figure, without a great deal of anxiety and stress. Reinforces me needing to keep quiet around authority like Nanna.).

_____

_____

_____

_____

_____

_____

_____

Another way to bring your limiting beliefs to the surface is to have a look at what consequences you've linked to breaking them. As humans, we typically only take action for two reasons: One is because there is a really compelling reward waiting for us when we achieve what we're going for, and the other is because there is a really awful consequence waiting for us if we don't. We are always motivated to move toward something perceived as good or away from something perceived as bad. Either way, good or bad, there's a consequence linked to the action.

You can get a look at your beliefs by identifying some of the consequences you have in place if you be, do, or have the things you say you want.

So think of something you'd like to be, do, or have that you've not yet had success with. Now, imagine actually having success with it. Really imagine this: Close your eyes and immerse yourself in the idea of having accomplished it. Notice the thoughts that accompany your success.

One example of this is quitting smoking. Often people wanting to quit smoking do this exercise and immediately, upon imagining they've quit smoking, start thinking that they're going to gain weight or that they can't possibly handle life's stress without smoking. The consequences to quitting smoking are gaining weight and not being able to manage the stress. This identifies situational beliefs that quitting smoking means a weight gain and inability to handle stress; we can also see the negative consequence they've linked to quitting smoking—namely that quitting smoking has the negative consequence of gaining weight. We also see the plus side they've attached to continuing to partake of the habit they say they want to quit—namely, that by smoking they are better able to handle stress. Therefore continuing to smoke prevents an unwanted weight gain and helps them manage stress.

I refer to this as the "If...then.... Therefore" way to find your beliefs.

In the space provided, list some of your "If...then.... Therefore" thoughts (e.g., **If** I become really wealthy, **then** my friends will be jealous and not associate with me. **Therefore** it's better to keep my finances just as they are so I don't lose my friends.).

_____

_____

_____

_____

_____

_____

_____

_____

One more round-about, yet highly effective way to identify your beliefs is to state the facts and then explain the meaning. Earlier I said that we live our lives by our beliefs. To expand on that slightly, consider that our lives become a mirrored reflection of our beliefs. Many people say "I need to see it to believe it," but if you play along and turn that one around, it tends to be a bit more accurate. You need to "believe it in order to see it."

For example, remember I mentioned we filter everything through our beliefs and apply the meaning that reinforces the belief. That applies to *everything* in our lives. Imagine for a moment that you have the belief that all women are bad drivers. So you're driving along one day en route to an appointment and on the highway you see a woman pulled over by the police. Without knowing any of the details, you likely store this as evidence to support your belief that all women are bad drivers because the cop has pulled one of those bad drivers over, and she probably deserved it.

Then as you continue on your way, you see an accident involving a few cars. You look over and notice that the very first car has a woman behind the wheel. Again, without knowing any of the details, you might conclude that the woman in the first car caused the accident; this again reinforces your belief.

Then you exit the highway, slightly behind schedule due to the accident that woman caused. You check your watch and think that if you just pick up the pace a bit you'll still make the meeting. As you approach the last light before your destination, it turns yellow. The car in front of you stops hard, and you don't quite make it as you wanted to scoot through on the yellow. Your tires screech as you slow to a stop but you still hit bumpers. Crap! You get out to see the damage and, sure enough, it's a flippin' woman driving the car ahead of you just who caused this.

Now, suppose you are a female driver and you have a belief that women are very good drivers among a sea of crazy drivers. Same scenario: You see the woman pulled over on the highway and perhaps you think, "I bet some jerk hit that poor woman and sped off."

Then you see the woman in the first car of the multi-car accident and perhaps you think, "See, that woman probably stopped in good time, and those other two careless drivers were probably tailgating and hit her."

And as you bump the bumper of the woman in front of you, you get out, very apologetic, saying that you shouldn't have been rushing and you're so sorry that you caused this. And all the while you're thinking that of course she should have stopped. That was the right thing to do, and you knew it.

These two examples illustrate how we take in the day-to-day events of our life and they get filtered through our existing beliefs to reinforce the truth of the belief, whether or not we even have all the information. This is going on without us even realizing it all day long.

Another way to "surface up" our beliefs is by looking at how we describe what's going on in our lives and then defining what we've made it mean, because your life experience and the meanings you assign (which are usually indicated by what you feel about it) are always mirroring your beliefs back to you.

To get an idea of what your beliefs are, in the space provided or in your journal, describe the current situations in your life, including what you're feeling about them. Then ask, "What belief must I have in place such that I'm experiencing it this way?" (e.g., I'm working at a job that I really hate going to. In order to be experiencing it this way I must have a belief in place that says "work is supposed to be hard and dreary.")

_____

_____

_____

_____

_____

_____

_____

## Blockages

In order to live our lives and make our beliefs come true, we also have another built-in system to reinforce them. These are also often the very things you heard when you were young. Other names for these blockages, which really call them what they are, are reasons, excuses, and justifications.

Whenever you find yourself defending or giving reasons or excuses for why you aren't being, doing, or having the things you want, this is a really big clue that you're up against a limiting belief and you've put a blockage in place to reinforce it. These reasons, excuses, and justifications are easy enough to identify, as they usually come in the form of the following statements with the blanks filled in with whatever it is you typically say you want:

**I can't** _____.

**I shouldn't** _____.

**I don't really want to** _____.

**I'm too (old, young, big, small, etc.)** _____.

**In order to** _____,

**I'd need to** _____.

Almost always there is a big but or because thrown in as well. As in "**I would** _____, but _____" or **I can't** _____, because _____."

Take a moment and jot down some of the reasons, excuses, and justifications that you're using to reinforce your beliefs. And from there, see if you can name what the belief might be (e.g., I'm too old (young) to get my college degree. I have a belief in place that says people at my age can't go to college. It's too late for me. I'm not good enough.).

You CAN Get There From Here

I'm too _____ to be, do, or have _____.

Meaning/belief: _____
_____

I can't have _____, because _____.

Meaning/belief: _____
_____

I shouldn't _____, because _____.

Meaning/belief: _____
_____

I don't really want to _____, because _____.

Meaning/belief: _____
_____

In order to _____, I'd need to _____.

Meaning/belief: _____

_____

I didn't get _____, because

_____.

Meaning/belief: _____

_____

Some of the limiting beliefs I've seen time and again are:
- I don't deserve it.
- I'm not worthy.
- It's too much. (I won't be able to handle it.)
- I'm not smart enough.
- I'm too old (or too young).
- I'm too busy.
- I don't have the money.
- No one will support me.
- It will be hard.
- It's too scary.
- I'm not strong enough.
- It's too risky.
- It will take so long.
- It will create conflict with family/friends.
- It's not for people like me.
- It's in my genes.
- I won't be able to.
- I've never done (had) it before.

As you read over these, perhaps one or two resonated with you. That is, did any of them seem to feel familiar or feel like they were a fit for you? If they did, chances are that, if you give this a bit of thought, you'll come up with all kinds of stored "proof" in the form of memories that support the belief and hold it firmly in place. We'll refer to this again in an upcoming chapter, but, for now, if anything is coming up for you in this regard, make a note of it in your journal.

Ok, so that might have left you feeling rather deflated, but here's the deal. Just because your beliefs are in there and running the show (just like that elephant), all is not doom and gloom.

As I touched on earlier, they aren't as cemented in as we once believed. Funny that, research has proven that our belief about beliefs was even a limiting belief. How 'bout that?!

And this isn't the first time a collective belief held by the population has been "busted," so to speak. No, no, no. We bust universally accepted beliefs all the time.

For example, remember that pool I mentioned in Chapter 1 that I loved so much? Well, when it was built, many of the other girls were into sun-tanning. So while I did my swimming thing in the water, they would be lined up lying flat out on brightly colored towels all around the pool deck, slathered in baby oil and soaking up the rays.

In case you missed that, they weren't covered in sun block. No, not in those days. Back then it was none other than baby oil. The belief of the day was that drenching oneself in baby oil and lying out in the high-noon sun was the best thing to do on a hot summer day.

What about seat belts? During the Seventies, shoulder straps weren't even attached to the lap belt and, for the most part, in Mom's car anyway (and I'm sure in countless others) the shoulder strap spent its days tucked neatly into the hook above the doors, never unfolded to see the light of day. And what about passengers in the back seat? In those days, my sister and I bounced around and clowned around in the back seat completely unharnessed. Seat belts were considered mandatory from a manufacturing standpoint but completely optional for the driver and passengers.

Here's a big one for you: How about the Earth is flat? That commonly held and widely accepted belief ended up being busted, too.

So take heart. Beliefs can be updated once they are identified and the person holding them decides they want to update them and move on. I think the very spelling of the word beliefs is even a clue for us if we're considering having a closer look. Do you see the little clue word embedded right in the middle of word *beliefs* that tips us off about how true our beliefs must be? Here, how about now: beLIEfs.

I've heard it said many times "never argue for your limitations unless you intend to keep them." That's what your limiting beliefs are: limitations.

So if you're ready to set down the idea of arguing for your limitations and bust out of your current limiting belief patterns, hang on to your hat because this next part is where it gets sort of crazy.

> *The world is round and the place which may seem like the end may also be the beginning.*
>
> ~ Ivy Baker

# II

# The Bridge: Tools to Get You to Your Destination

*When you change the way you look at things, the things you look at change.*
~ Dr. Wayne Dyer

# Chapter 4

## The Law of Attraction as Child's Play

Did you ever play the "Hot and Cold" game as a kid? Now I don't know for sure if that's what it was called, but it went something like this: Two kids would set out to play the game. One would pick an object, typically something right out in plain view, but the one selecting the object wouldn't tell their friend what it was. Their role was to simply give clues to guide their friend to find the selected item.

The clues ranged from "warm" to "warmer" to "hot" and "you're on fire!" for indicating that the seeker was heading in the right direction. And to signal that they weren't, the clues ranged from "cold" to "colder" to "you're ice!" And, if I recall correctly, the description of the temperatures and the level of excitement or letdown in the tone of voice also played a key role in guiding the seeker.

The seeker in the game wandered around somewhat like a pinball in slow motion, stepping in one direction and waiting for the signal as to whether they should take their next step in the same direction or veer off in another direction. Once they got the signal, they would again step as guided and wait. When the temperature clues indicated they were on fire, they would scan the room and try to guess what the prized secret item was. I loved that game as a kid, and even today I play it with my son with lots of giggles and "let's play again" requests after each round.

The thing I've come to realize about that little game is that, aside from it being fun, it's pretty much a great comparison of how the Law of Attraction works—in the down-to-earth, tell-me-only-what-I-need-to-know way I like to explain things.

Now, I realize there is a tremendous amount of information out there about the Law of Attraction and the various other laws that work in conjunction with it, and if you're interested in studying this in depth, I encourage you to do so, as it's fascinating stuff. But for the sake of just having a working "need-to-know" knowledge, the following is the way I see it and the basics of how I teach it in comparison to the Hot and Cold kids' game.

The main difference between the Law of Attraction game and the Hot and Cold game is that, in the Law of Attraction game, you (the player) are playing a solo game and not dependent upon a partner for your clues.

So it goes something like this: In the kids' game, the object that is being sought is usually something within plain sight. In life, with the Law of Attraction, the item being sought is usually also something more or less within our sight, too. It's often a tangible item, or an upgrade or improvement to something we already have. It's the experiences and things we say we want to be, do, and have in our lives. And we can usually picture it in our mind's eye even if it's not physically in front of us.

Also, just like in the kids' game, there are clues to indicate we're getting closer, and there are clues to indicate we're heading away from the item.

And *this* is the interesting part: We are experiencing these clues all the time. You see, we human beings have a very advanced internal guidance system (it's the equivalent of those "hot" and "cold" clues; it even has all the gradations that we mimicked as kids by embellishing just how hot or cold our playmate was), and it's built right into each and every one of us. This clue mechanism is none other than our own feelings. Yep, good ol' feelings, emotions, and "gut reactions" are the clues in the Law of Attraction game of our lives that guide us toward or away from what we want.

I know that's a very simplistic take on a very complex topic, but, as I said, it's a tell you-what-you-need-to-know-so-you-can-use-it-right-now approach.

So, how does this game work? Well, imagine that you're walking about your life searching for the experiences and things you want to be, do, and have, to create feelings of success and happiness.

Also imagine that everywhere you go, off in the distance, both to your left and right, are neon signs that say, "Welcome. Please come in." These welcome signs are hanging on two open doors. It doesn't matter where you go or what you do; these two doors with the welcome signs are always there off in the distance, and they're both always open.

Behind one of these doors are all the tangible items you've ever wanted and all the feelings of love, joy, success, happiness, peace, and every wonderful feeling you've ever had the delight to experience or even dreamed of one day experiencing. This door is truly the door to bliss.

The other door, on the other hand, isn't one that you want to go through. It's filled with all the tangible items you've ever had and cursed—that lemon of a car, the broken bicycle, that one job that was the worst of 'em all, etc.—and the feelings behind that door are fear, sadness, anger, despair, and on and on it goes. This is an awful kind of place, and you really don't want to go there. We'll call this the door to misery.

So as you go about living your life with these two metaphorical doors always with you off in the distance on either side, with each interaction you have, each activity you take part in, and each conversation with others (or yourself), what you feel in each moment is an indicator of which door you're walking toward (or through).

Pretty neat, wouldn't you say? As we bounce along through our life playing this crazy game of the Law of Attraction, we can tell in any given moment if we're "hot" or "cold" with regard to getting what we really want by checking in with how we feel.

Think about this for a moment. Have you ever been in what you considered an "awful" situation and felt joyous? Or, have you ever been in what you consider an amazing situation and felt miserable?

Or even, have you ever been "steam coming out of your ears" angry and been beaming from ear to ear with a truly happy smile?

Not likely! We're simply not wired that way as humans.

And *this*, by the way, is one of those times when I know it's a bit out there, but, if you're willing, play along and let this swirl around your thoughts....

As humans, we're actually spiritual beings having a human experience, even though we often think we're human beings having a spiritual experience. When your spirit is birthed into the human form called you, it puts on what I call its "human suit" (your body and mind) and begins the journey called your life. This human suit serves as your spirit's "vehicle" for your journey. This vehicle (your body and mind) comes with all the latest bells and whistles, just like any new vehicle does.

So the bodies that you and I are zooming around in have built-in signaling systems. The signals (like the "hot" and "cold" clues in the game) show up as our feelings, and they indicate which direction our spirit would like the body to go in to keep both the body and the spirit, happy.

The problem is that, as humans, we don't come with a handbook to explain all the signal clues, so we sometimes label the feeling signals themselves as the problem. So while we typically embrace the feelings and emotions that are pleasant and enjoy basking in these, usually we shy away from the darker ones and often do our best to "pretend" them away—as in, we pretend they don't matter, we pretend they don't hurt, we pretend they don't bother us, and we even pretend they're not there and not affecting us at all, and we ignore them.

But, just like I think most of us know that nothing good can come from ignoring the warning signals that show up on the dash of your car, the same is true here with your feeling signals.

That's because your feelings serve a fundamental purpose, and they aren't something to ignore or pretend away. They are your body's high-tech signaling system designed to guide you to all the people, places, and things that will result in the happiness you are seeking.

Imagine what your life might be like if, from this point onward, rather than considering your feelings and emotions as something annoying, or something to be ignored or suppressed, you embraced them—and I mean *all* of them—for the wonderful "hot" and "cold" clues that they are. They are the signals that tell you if you're heading in the right direction or if you need to adjust your course.

By seeing your emotions and feelings this way, you will be playing the game of the Law of Attraction with greater awareness than before. In other words, you lock on to those positive feelings you encounter while actively living your life to have them steer you to the things you want to be do and have.

*And* you'll be able to recognize, accept, and honor the negative or darker feelings that come up, too. You'll easily accept these as nothing to shy away from because they, too, are signals telling you that by continuing to think, do, or take part in what you are currently thinking or doing, you are heading straight toward that "misery door" and directly to all things you don't want. Further, by continuing on in this direction of ignoring or trying to suppress the darker feelings, you're actually moving yourself further and further away from that "bliss door" that holds all the things you do want.

That's a very basic overview of the Law of Attraction. If you incorporate this alone into your life, you will experience different results than you did by just passing your feelings and emotions off at the surface level.

*But,* I want to take you a step further.

## You Simply Can't Make a Square Peg Fit Through a Round Hole!

When my son was very young, he, like many toddlers, had one of those shape sorter games. Ty's had all the typical characteristics: bright colors, a sturdy bucket, blocks in a variety of shapes, and the all-important slotted lid that, once affixed to the bucket, was used to sort the shapes to get them into the bucket: star shapes through the star slot, square shapes through the square slot, circle shapes through the circle slot, and triangle shapes through the triangle slot. This was the only way to get the shapes into the bucket with the lid on. No variations worked—*ever*!

Ty played with this thing often, and each time he did he would sit there intent on trying to get the shapes he chose through the holes he wanted. When it happened, which was more often than not in the early days, that he chose a shape that didn't match the slot, my darling Angel's spirited determination would appear. With increasing concentration and force, he would pound the square block to make it fit through the round hole. After several unsuccessful tries, one of a few things would usually happen: He would throw the block, he would kick the bucket over, or he would give up and go on to something else, be it another shape or another activity altogether. The thing is that, even with all the determination and force he could muster, he could never get a mismatched shape through the slotted lid *ever*!

I didn't slip in this story simply as a way to talk about my son. I'm telling you it because it also helps explain how the Law of Attraction works. It's like this: If you think of the things you want to be, do, and have (all that great stuff that's through the "bliss door") like the various shaped blocks, then your feelings and emotions (your guidance signals) would be the slotted lid in this little shape-sorter game.

So even if you muster up the same determination and persistence that my son used, if your feelings are not a match for the things you are wanting, the things you are wanting will not fit through the slot and reach you.

A real-world example to illustrate this is to suppose you want to experience financial abundance. You can picture it clearly in your head; the vision might be that of your bank statement coming in with a nice, big, juicy bank balance at the bottom. This would be the square-shaped block.

In reality, suppose your bank balance is currently in overdraft, and you have a panicky, sick feeling in the pit of your stomach because you can't see how to turn it around. That feeling that you get represents the shape on this lid. In this example, that panicky, sick feeling could be the round hole in the slotted lid.

No matter how much you want that juicy bank balance that you can picture so clearly in your head, the reality is that the thoughts of bank balances right now create an icky feeling for you. The picture in your head and the feeling you feel simply aren't a match. As long as this is the case, you will be no more successful in attaining (or maintaining) this juicy bank balance than my son was at putting the square block through the round hole.

This is the precise trouble many people have when attempting to "do" the Law of Attraction. Just like the reactions my son had, many folks, after trying this unsuccessfully a few times, get so frustrated with the whole idea that they eventually just throw things and give up. OK, maybe not about the throwing things part, but you get the point. Who wants to keep playing when the game doesn't work the way we want it to and we can't figure out how to win?

## OK, So Enough of These Games: The Universe Has a Job to Do

Consider that the Universe (or God, or the Divine, or whatever name you use for the all-loving, abundant creative force from which everything flows) has one job and one job only. Its only job is to match the signals it receives and respond with more items to feel the same way about. That's it. One job and one job only. It matches signals. It doesn't translate; it doesn't interpret; it doesn't have favorites, it doesn't rest—365/24/7 it matches signals. *Period!*

Here's how that previous example might look without flowing it through the game comparison and just using Law of Attraction language. Suppose you want to manifest financial abundance. You start to imagine that juicy bank balance, and this time thoughts of your bills come to mind. The thoughts that also come to you are "Every penny is already spent, and there's nothing left. How will I ever get ahead of the game to get that balance?" The feelings you are experiencing in conjunction with these thoughts are feelings of hopelessness and discouragement. These feelings (signals) are sent out to the Universe without you even lifting a finger or doing anything else, and they are picked up.

The Universe reads the signals and responds by supplying you with people, places, or things that serve to match the feelings of hopelessness and discouragement that you sent with your thoughts and feelings. It matches your feelings and thoughts with items that will give you the opportunity to feel exactly the way you did with the signal you sent.

Did you get that? The Universe doesn't give a hoot about what you are attempting to experience (or manifest). Its *only* job is to match the signals it receives and respond with situations that will create the exact same feelings for you. The signal you sent, despite what you were trying to do, is a signal of hopelessness and discouragement. So *this* is all that the Universe can send back to you, because its only job is to match.

So in the very moment you were attempting to bring wealth to yourself, based on your true thoughts and feelings, you unintentionally sent a request out to the Universe—a signal to match your feelings and send you more stuff to feel exactly the same way about. It doesn't send what you were trying for; it can only send a match to what you were truly emitting.

Another key element of the Law of Attraction is that it's working all the time—as in 365/24/7—whether we're thinking about it or not.

An example of the Law of Attraction working when we're not even consciously trying is this: Have you ever been fuming mad at your spouse or a friend, but the person was important to you so you wanted to patch things up? So despite your anger, you initiate a conversation. Things start off OK, but then take a slight turn, and from there it goes downhill *fast*. Tempers flare and awful things are said, and it turns into the verbal equivalent of a "knock-down-drag-'em-out brawl." This, again, is the Universe matching your true feelings.

Logically you wanted to sort things out. But at the feeling level, the level that the Law of Attraction matches and responds to, you entered into the conversation fuming mad. So in turn, you attracted more situations to feel fuming mad about and—wouldn't you know it?—that very conversation you were in the midst of gave you exactly that.

My point in going over this in so many ways is to hopefully win you over to considering that your *feelings*, and I mean *all* of them, are really what are determining what you're experiencing in your life.

As I've mentioned, the Universe is matching your feelings 365/24/7, and there is no pause button. If you're sitting reading this book intrigued and excited as you grasp this information, the Universe is matching. If you're watching the evening news about violence and tragedies and feeling things like outrage, discouragement, and hopelessness, the Universe is matching. If you're in the midst of a heated argument, the Universe is matching. If you're stuck in traffic somewhere getting more stressed by the second, the Universe is matching. If you're walking hand in hand on a beach with your spouse basking in feelings of peace and love, the Universe is matching. If you're working in a job you love and feeling appreciated and inspired, the Universe is matching. No pauses, no breaks, no time off *ever*—just matching, matching, matching, 365/24/7 matching.

Knowing that there are no pauses, even when you're in the midst of upheavals and challenges, one of the greatest gifts you could give yourself is to make peace with your emotions. Rather than vilify them or even try to pretend them away, try on the idea and practice of welcoming them with open arms, so to speak, because they are the clues as to what's "coming down the pike" for you.

Allow yourself to simply acknowledge and accept what you're really feeling. When you have challenges to attend to, and your feelings are not great, take steps to get yourself into a better feeling state *before* you tackle the challenging task or discussion.

This action of noticing and then managing your feelings (when they are not what you would like them to be) is called "breaking state"—as in, breaking or ending the emotional state you're in. The idea is that you can't change something unless you notice it. So notice what you're feeling. Come off auto-pilot with regard to your feelings. Notice them, and consciously decide if you like how you feel or if you don't like how you feel. In any moment have your intention for your feelings become "I want to feel good, and head to the 'bliss door,'" because your feelings are the key to how your life is unfolding.

In that moment when things are stressful, or you're angry or hurt, or whatever other unpleasant emotion you are experiencing, and you have a challenge to take care of, take action by accepting that you can change your state before taking your next step. We have become so used to doing things and expecting things instantly that many of us have forgotten that we really can stop to "collect our thoughts" or, in this case, "collect and upgrade our feelings" before taking action.

Once you have lifted your feelings up a bit, you will be coming at the challenge from a more empowered or inspired state, and also you'll be sending a more desirable signal. From here, chances of a satisfactory, or even great, outcome are dramatically increased. Because 365/24/7, no exceptions, it is always your *true* feelings, in the moment, that are being matched. Regardless of the situations you are in, your feelings are what count as the matching signals.

As we saw with the examples of the finances and the argument, what you intend isn't what counts here; it's what you're feeling. So adjust your feelings before taking action to increase your chances of achieving the results you're looking for.

> *You can never solve a problem at the same level of consciousness that created it.*
>
> ~ Albert Einstein

## State Breaking Habits

The following are simple ways to quickly (and temporarily) get yourself out of a "funk" or negative place, so that you can go from sending a feeling lousy signal to the Universe back to sending a feeling good signal.

1. Play "Stop and Switch." This is a fun thing to do, and I recommend you do on paper as well as just in your head. The idea is to stop the negative thoughts and feelings about the situation as quickly as you notice you're thinking and feeling them, and switch them with thoughts of what you do want to experience instead. For example, suppose you're standing in a grocery line and all the other lines seem to be moving while yours is not. You catch yourself beginning to fume

and say in your head, "OK, so this is what I don't want to be experiencing. So what would I rather experience?" Then list off in your thoughts what you would like to have as your experience in this line. For example, "I would like my line to begin zooming faster than all the others," "I would like another cashier to open and signal me to come right up," or "I would like to enjoy this apparent delay." Get creative and play with this. I've had mind-blowing results playing this game in my head and even more powerful results when I did it on paper with bigger things.

2. Another variation of this is "Wouldn't it be nice if…?" Same idea: When you're in the midst of something you don't want, say, "Wouldn't it be nice if…?" Allow your thoughts to swirl around all the wonderful things that this situation could be improved with. This is another one to do in your journal when you have a moment.

3. Keep an appreciation/gratitude list or journal and add to it with a minimum of five entries daily. When you need a quick pick-me-up, either re-read from your list or, if you're on the fly and don't have your journal handy, think about and recite some of the things you're grateful for.

4. Take a moment to play your favorite, most uplifting, music and even sing along. Better yet, dance and sing along, giving it your all—you know, as they say, "like no one's watching." I do this singing routine in my car, and I'm sure I've given a stressed-out driver or two something to laugh at as they glance over to my car and witness my enthusiasm! And this leads to…

5. Do a random act of kindness. There's nothing like seeing someone else light up because of some kind act you've done in part to make your own spirits soar.

6. Watch or listen to something funny. There's nothing like a good belly laugh to break you out of a funk. I have a couple of clips on my computer and, when I get all intense, I play them. It doesn't matter how many times I've seen them. I still crack up.

7. Hug someone you love, or ask someone you love for a hug. I'm a raving fan of hugs, and one of my favorite things is turning ughs to hugs!

These are just a few of the things you can easily do to pick yourself up when you're feeling down. Feeling better will send a much more desirable signal off to the Universe for it to match.

These, in and of themselves, won't completely change your feelings, beliefs, or any of the other things that we've talked about that might be holding you back from the things you want in life.

But there is something that will. It's a little out there (*way* out there actually), but take a leap of faith and come along for the ride of your life!

> *When you have come to the edge of all light that you know and are about to drop off into the darkness of the unknown, Faith is knowing one of two things will happen: there will be something solid to stand on or you will be taught to fly.*
>
> ~ Patrick Overton

# Chapter 5

## Tapping: EFT & MTT; A Funny Thing Happened

A funny thing happened when I was studying the Law of Attraction.
In the early days after my son was born, I was an independent consultant rather than an employee on maternity leave, so even in that first year there was much "day job" work to be done. The majority of this work was in the area of finance, but all could be done from my home office and at my own pace, which usually meant when the baby was sleeping. During this time, I was also learning more and more about the Law of Attraction. Again, to suit my "work when the baby is sleeping" schedule, my Law of Attraction studies were mostly through home-study programs and other means of independent study.

So on a typical day, when Ty napped I worked. My office was set up as Multi-tasking-zilla Zone: main computer and my desk for the day-job tasks, a smaller desk (made from a stack of over-stuffed bankers' boxes) with my laptop perched on top was the "training and studying" area, and a clear path to the office door for quick exits for when the baby woke!

One day, when I was listening to the pre-recorded Law of Attraction material, I kept hearing this talk about EFT. Each time I heard this, it sent off a "does not compute" jolt in me because, being involved in finance, this just didn't seem to fit. You see, in finance, I had come to know very well that the acronym EFT stood for electronic funds transfer.

So, as you might have suspected, the first time it happened, I thought I should just shut everything down and have a nap myself. But, I persisted. Then, a few days later, I was listening to a completely different Law of Attraction expert, and there it was again. Only that time, they were introducing an interview with an EFT practitioner as part of our lesson. I decided to shut down the finance stuff for the day and listen in to see how, exactly, electronic funds transfers fit into the world of the Law of Attraction. (I was also hoping it was the formula to having funds transferred electronically into my account!)

The interview started, and it was surprisingly interesting. And who knew? In the world of the Law of Attraction, EFT wasn't about finance or funds at all!

It was about this wacky "energy healing tapping thing" called the Emotional Freedom Technique. Well, the stuff they talked about in the interview was interesting, but my skeptical, analytical nature didn't quite buy it. I recall saying a bunch of "yeah rights" and "who are you kiddings?" The interview carried on, and when it ended I just sat there like I was in a trance. It had all sounded fascinating, and the optimistic "try anything once" side of me simply *had* to know more. Skepticism aside, could what they were saying be true?

In the days that followed, after Googling away, I found the "EFT Site." I read lots of info and articles, and then found "the manual" they had referred to in the interview. And, get this: It was a free download! Now, I appreciate free stuff as much as the next person, but, in this case, this only served to fuel my skepticism. Anything as good as what they were describing certainly couldn't be summed up and served up as a free manual.

I printed a copy and began reading. My initial reaction was surprisingly one of outrage! How could what they were describing work? I was convinced it was all an elaborate scam. I was determined; I would try it on the years of "painful stuff" I was still working through and, when it didn't work, then *I would be the one to de-bunk them.* I would somehow make it right that these EFT people stopped talking all this nonsense.

So with the manual on my lap and my own spirited determination fully engaged, I followed the steps as they were presented, and I worked on the awful fight I had just had a few days before. Every time I even thought about that fight, I got very mad and very sad all at the same time. Maybe you know that feeling. You want to cry and beat the crap out of something simultaneously.

So there I sat doing what the manual said, tapping my hand, tapping my face, and thinking about that awful fight, following along, step by step, and within a few minutes I was neither mad nor sad. In fact, I was good! *What???* I was *good.* How the heck could that be?!

"OK," I thought. "So maybe I was just over it already. Maybe I wasn't as mad or sad as I thought I was." Maybe this tapping had nothing to do with how peaceful I was feeling about it right then, so I decided to try it on something else. I went for a big one this time: I decided to do the tapping thing on a major fallout I had had with my mom right before I left home. This one was off the Richter scale for how much it upset me, even all these years later. Same deal: manual on lap, follow the steps...and *same deal!* After just a few minutes, I was totally OK. I couldn't even get myself upset by trying.

"Holy crap," I thought. "That's crazy and cool, and I can't believe that just happened!"

Let me tell you: I gave up all notions of debunking them. I jumped ship on that plan totally. I was like a woman possessed. I had to know everything, learn everything, and totally master this crazy tapping thing called EFT.

Months later I was still loving it, and practicing and learning all I could. I had cleared years and years worth of "dark painful gunk" that I had been carrying around. Much of it was even stuff I had thought I had "dealt with already." Friends and family would almost hide when they saw me coming because I wanted to tap on everyone I knew. I started offering mere acquaintances the opportunity to have a free tapping session just so I could practice more.

Well, that was around five years ago, and I'm still tapping on myself and with anyone else who's interested. And, it's because of the profound impact EFT has had on my life, and on the lives of my friends, family, and clients, that I'm so thrilled to share the basics of it with you in this book. I hope you'll try it, even amid skepticism, so that you will experience the profound, life-changing results that using this crazy tapping technique can bring about.

But before going into the specifics of how to do EFT, I'll tell you a little about what this wacky "energy healing tapping" thing is.

Thousands of years ago, the Chinese discovered a life-force energy, (chi), that flows within each of us. This energy flows along a series of pathways called meridians, similar to the way our blood travels through our body via our veins and arteries. These meridians are the very pathways that are treated with the more widely known acupuncture and acupressure.

When our energy is flowing smoothly, we feel what might be called a neutral or positive emotion. But when we feel a recurring or excessive negative emotion, it is the result of a blockage along one of these energy meridians. (A point to note here is that this experience of an excessive negative emotion is not the same as having a typical emotional reaction to a life situation. For example, it is expected you will grieve at the passing of a loved one. But still grieving two years later and not being able to move beyond your grief is one example of the type of excessive negative emotion I'm referring to. Another is feeling intense anxiety in an everyday situation that others don't seem as bothered by.)

Now fast-forward a bit to 1991. This is when a Stanford Engineer named Gary Craig was studying a meridian-based healing system with Dr. Roger Callahan. By 1995, Gary Craig had transformed and simplified the fascinating procedures he had learned into a new procedure that just about anyone could self-administer. He called his simplified version of this amazing meridian-based healing the Emotional Freedom Technique, and EFT was born.

The premise of EFT is simply this: The cause of all negative emotion is a disruption in the body's energy system.

When the energy blockage is not dealt with, or neutralized, the emotion intensifies. If the emotion continues to intensify unchecked, it will usually show up in the body as physical pain or illness. And according to an increasing range of sources, there is an underlying emotional issue behind all physical ailments in the body.

To address the blockage, we can perform EFT by identifying the issue (memory or pain) causing the blockage and then stimulating the meridians by gently tapping on several key points along the meridians located in the hands, face, and upper body.

Once the tapping is done successfully, the blockage is neutralized and the energy flow is restored. The negative emotion (or physical pain) is released. Usually permanently!

In plain English, if you think of this series of energy meridians as a series of roads and highways, all the vehicles traveling along the roads represent the free-flowing energy within us. If there is a blockage on the highway (think of a stopped car or an accident during rush hour), at first it's not too bad, but as time passes, if it's not cleared up, the highway becomes congested, and traffic can't flow freely. As more time passes, the congestion worsens and traffic can even grind to a halt.

This is essentially what happens on an energetic level in our bodies. Rather than a traffic jam, the blockage shows up as an emotional or physical ailment such as:

- Anxiety,
- Excessive stress,
- Panic attacks,
- Excessive fears,
- Self-worth or self-esteem issues,
- Abuse trauma,
- Excessive grief,
- Addictive and compulsive behaviors,
- Listlessness or feelings of intense sadness,
- Self-confidence issues,
- Migraine headaches,
- Chronic fatigue,
- Excessive anger,
- Emotional eating,
- Insomnia,
- And many others.

In the case of our roads and highways, preventing and removing blockages to ensure smooth-flowing traffic is a widely accepted principle. We have all sorts of measures in place to minimize the blockages and clear them up as quickly as possible when they do occur.

Now, thanks to the efforts of Gary Craig, we can use this amazing tool called EFT to address and clear the energetic blockages resulting in our emotional and physical discomforts.

We can even address the items locked away in our subconscious, as well as those limiting beliefs we've been identifying. EFT is truly a modern-day miracle. As is said in the tapping community, "Try it on everything!"

In the pages that follow, I will share the basics of EFT, plus some creative variations of other Meridian Tapping Techniques (MTT for short) that go beyond what is covered by the basic EFT routine. By no means is this the extent of EFT or MTT. It is merely the basics of the basics to give you a working knowledge so you can try it for yourself. If you wish to study EFT in more detail, I encourage you to do so. For the purposes of this book, as mentioned in the beginning of the book, by taking part and practicing EFT yourself following the steps I outline, you are in agreement that you are taking full responsibility for your own health and well-being. If you would like to go beyond what I've summarized here and work at a deeper level, I also encourage you to seek out a trained, qualified practitioner to work with you. But even just by doing the basics, you will likely be amazed and empowered by the results you can achieve on your own.

EFT can be used very effectively right when you are in the moment of something troubling, as well as for recalling painful memories and tapping on them to release the painful feelings associated with the memory. It can be used to very gently release your attachment to those limiting beliefs we've been talking about so that new, more empowering, updated beliefs can take their place.

I will start by giving you all the relevant info, and then bring it all together for you and offer a couple of tapping round examples, suggestions, and a little project to get you well on your way.

You might want to read through this section completely once to get the big picture, and then come back and go through it again while trying it.

## The Tapping Points

The basic EFT process I use involves the EFT shortcut and works with the following points:

KC—Karate Chop (for the set-up)

EB—Eyebrow

SE—Side of the Eye

UE—Under Eye

UN—Under Nose

CH—Chin

CB—Collarbone

UA—Under Arm

TH—Top of Head

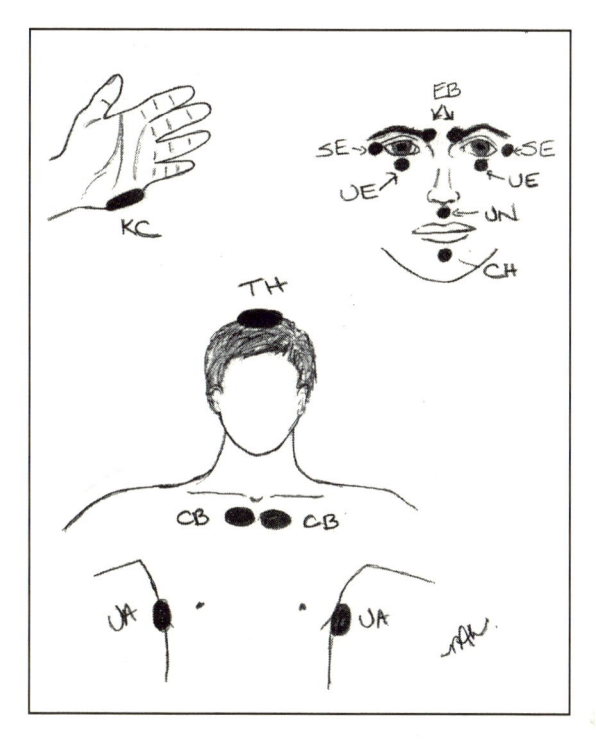

When performing EFT, you will stimulate these points, in the order presented, by gently tapping with the finger tips of your index and middle fingers (using about the same pressure as you'd use to strum your fingers on a desk). Each point gets tapped about seven to ten times.

## The Importance of Specifics

In my earlier comparison to the blockage being like a car pulled over on the highway, if we were going to call in for help for this car, we wouldn't be very effective if we simply reported the problem as "a car on the highway," or even if we added that "it's a green car." This description is just too general; the authorities wouldn't have a clue where we wanted the help to go. We would need to narrow it down quite a bit, and tell which highway and where on that highway it was. Perhaps the description would sound something like "it's a green car in the northbound lanes of Highway 400, just past the exit for or Highway 89." This specific information zeroes right in on where the problem is so help can be dispatched directly to the where it's needed.

The same is true for EFT. Just as we needed to be specific to get help to the cause of the blockage on the highway, we need to be very specific with the incident we are working on in EFT to achieve the best results. This is one of the key points I stress with EFT. If you are working on too general an issue, your results will be inconsistent. Sometimes it will "work" and sometimes not—just as maybe the authorities could get help out to the correct area from the first vague description, but likely not.

One way to zone right in on the blockage is by tapping right in the moment of discomfort (or by recording the details of the troubling event in a journal so that you can do the tapping later). For example, suppose you have an argument. You would want to tap as soon as possible afterward or jot the details down in your journal to tap on later when you can.

Or, if you're dealing with memories of events from a long time ago, you would want to be sure to focus on a specific event as opposed to a global feeling. You can tell if something is global or specific by identifying it and then asking yourself if it describes only one memory, or if it's more of a heading under which several memories could be noted. If it's only one memory, then it's likely specific enough. If, however, there could be many memories that all fit under that general heading, then you will want to narrow it down more to each of the individual memories.

For example, if I wanted to tap on "I'm not good enough" I would ask myself if this brought up only one memory or many. In this case, a whole lot of memories could fit under this heading, so I'm pretty certain it's a global issue. So, I would isolate some of those memories to get to the specifics. In this case suppose I came up with "feeling so hurt that time Mom asked why I didn't get first place when I told her I won second place in the national art competition." Now *that* is a specific incident that's tappable.

I suggest a technique called the "Movie Technique" to distill global events down to the specifics to work on.

## Movie Technique

After you've chosen an area of focus to work on (this is like that "heading" I mentioned before), distill it down further to the equivalent of a trailer for a movie: a short summary with the all-important *"bang"* scene that is the precise moment the negative feeling was triggered.

Then give the movie a title (just a few words that represent the feeling and a short reminder description of the situation). The above example shows this. The movie title for this example could be "Feeling So Hurt When Mom Criticized Me for Not Winning First Place."

This movie title is relevant because, with those few words, we summarize the feeling and a brief description called a "reminder phrase" of when the feeling happened. We use this reminder phrase while doing the tapping. It notes the feeling and a short description of the specific incident so we stay "tuned in" while doing our round of EFT to release the discomfort from the memory.

## Intensity Ratings 0–10

Before beginning each EFT tapping round, it's important to rate the level of discomfort or the intensity of the negative feeling about whatever it is we are trying to release.

0 is nothing and 10 is extreme intensity or discomfort.

This rating gives you a starting point, shows your progress, and indicates when the issue is resolved.

It's also helpful in letting you know you've switched "aspects" when working on an issue.

## Aspects

As you're working through or "releasing" an issue, you may notice the movie starts to change and/or you may have different feelings come up. For instance, you could start with a very sad movie, and partway through you start feeling angry about it and there doesn't seem to be any sadness left.

This is usually an indicator that you're making progress and that you've touched upon a new layer or "aspect" of the issue.

Once you're aware of this new aspect, and if/when the intensity of the first movie is low (3 or less), rename the movie accordingly, start a new round from the set-up with this new movie, and work through the process.

Using the previous example, after tapping on the feeling of being hurt, perhaps the movie changed and feelings of anger toward my mom came up. I would honor and accept my feelings by not trying to feel (or pretend I felt) something that I thought more appropriate. In this process, we simply accept that what we're feeling is what we're getting as a clue from our subconscious to clear next. So I'd rename the movie "Feeling So Angry at My Mom for Criticizing Me About Not Winning First Place," re-rate the intensity, and begin another round of tapping.

Keep working through issues getting the intensity down as low as possible for each before moving on.

## The Set-Up

For many of us, we have attempted to change our behavior and "get over" much of what's holding us back for as long as we can remember.

Sometimes we have success and sometimes we don't. When we don't have success with this "changing," it's usually because the subconscious has no plan of letting go or changing.

As you'll likely recall from earlier chapters, the subconscious has everything stored away, in those files marked "this is good—do more" or "this is bad—stop immediately," with the primary objective of keeping us safe, all from the perspective of a newborn to a 7-year-old. The trouble with this is that, although we say we now want to do things differently, the original files of experiences and beliefs about what is in our best interest from a perspective of safety, are the ones ruling the show—just like it was in our elephant story with the elephant in charge no matter what the rider wanted.

Even though at a conscious level we've grown and moved on (hence wanting the change now), at the subconscious level changing possibly equals doing something that threatens our very safety.

When a part of us wants to change but we keep "sabotaging" ourselves, or making small changes and then sliding back or having results that are less that we wanted, it's because the subconscious is not in agreement with the change.

If we don't get permission from our subconscious, EFT, like everything else, may not work because of this. This is a basic description of something called psychological reversal. "Psychological reversal" is a fancy term meaning that our core belief, based largely upon our experiences and the things we absorbed up to age 7, is so strong against whatever we are trying to do that, no matter how much we consciously say we want something, we will subconsciously over-rule and prevent it every time. This is the equivalent of that elephant stomping to the right no matter how much the rider tried to get him to go left.

So the set-up is a way to get in touch with our subconscious and get it to let us in or "give us permission" to address the issue, even when there's a contradictory core belief behind it.

And although psychological reversal isn't always present, EFT will not be effective if it is and we don't address it, so we always assume it is present and start every round of EFT with a set-up (or remaining issue set-up).

As you'll see from the details that follow, performing the set-up involves tapping on the Karate Chop point on the side of the hand.

As I like to point out, when you shake someone's hand, your fingertips rest on their Karate Chop point, and their fingers rest on yours. I think of the set-up tapping as if we're shaking hands with the subconscious to show that this is a friendly undertaking and one that is in our best interest.

## Performing the Set-Up

While tapping with two or three fingers of one hand on the Karate Chop point of the other (see the diagram of Tapping Points, on page 81), repeat the following set-up phrase (or remaining issue set-up phrase) three times.

**Set-up phrase**: "Even though I have this (insert movie title), I deeply and completely love and accept myself."

**Remaining issue set-up phrase**: "Even though **I still have some of this** (insert movie title), I deeply and completely love and accept myself."

Note: In working with many clients, I've found that for many people, even just saying "I deeply and completely love and accept myself" brings up all kinds of emotion and even tears. If this happens for you, try humming the phrase until you are able to say it with words. Also, in this instance, I always suggest doing some journaling about your feelings when you say this statement, as this will likely provide insight into some of your beliefs about self-worth and deservingness, and these will be keys for you to work on with this process.

## The Process

Once you've done your set-up (or remaining set-up, if you're doing an additional round on the same issue), you go right on to the tapping.

Starting at the Eyebrow point, working downward through the face points to the Collarbone and Under Arm, and ending with the Top of Head point, tap each point approximately seven to ten times while saying the reminder phrase (the movie title used in the set-up). You can tap on either side of the body and tap with either hand.

Once you've completed a full round (the set-up three times and then tapped through all the points), take a deep breath in through your nose and exhale through your mouth. I also often suggest taking a sip of water between rounds.

Then re-rate the issue on the same scale of 0–10

Take a moment also to jot down any new thoughts or feelings that come to you that you might also tap on.

Usually, even after one round, there will be downward movement on the discomfort scale. Sometimes it will even be dramatically reduced after just one round. But in the event that the rating does not come down to 0, and you want to continue working on this issue, re-rate the issue and do another round, starting with the "remaining issue set-up phrase."

Continue working on the same issue until the intensity is a 0, which can often happen in a few rounds!

## Testing Your Work

Once you've gotten the rating down, to be certain the intensity level has gone down and will stay down, you need to test it by trying to get the intensity back up. To do this, imagine the memory as vividly as possible. Imagine it brighter, feel it more intensely, have the sounds involved become louder—do whatever you can to get the intensity back up. Just like I talked about when I first discovered EFT, I tried my darndest to get myself upset again when thinking about the memory I was tapping for, but I couldn't.

If you can get it to come back up, this simply means there's still more to be done on this issue. So, start again by identifying the feeling and creating a movie. Work through again with what has come up until you get it back down to a 0 and it remains at a 0 no matter how you try to get any intensity to come up again.

When you are certain you cannot get the intensity back up on the original issue, you can likely conclude that the issue is resolved and move on to another issue or another aspect of this one.

Here's an example to tie it all together:

I want to do some tapping, so I get a glass of water. (Being well hydrated is not just great for your overall health, but energy healing works much better in a well-hydrated body.) I get my journal handy to jot down any thoughts and feelings that come up while I'm tapping, and I begin.

I select the area of focus (which may turn out to be a global heading requiring that I distill it down further to a specific painful memory to work on and create a movie title from). In this example, let's use that same area of focus stated as "I'm not good enough" and say I distilled it down to the movie title "Feeling So Hurt When Mom Criticized Me for Not Winning First Place."

I rate the intensity as a 10 for how hurt I was.

Here's a "worksheet" to use for the process:

Identify an area of focus: _____

Movie Title: _____

Rating: _____

Thoughts or New Aspects: _____

_____

_____

And I begin tapping. (Feel free to look at the diagram until you memorize the points.)

I do the set-up three times as follows:

Tapping on the **Karate Chop point**, I say: "Even though I felt so hurt when Mom criticized me for not winning first place, I deeply and completely love and accept myself."

Still tapping on the **Karate Chop point,** I again say: "Even though I felt so hurt when Mom criticized me for not winning first place, I deeply and completely love and accept myself."

And a third time while still tapping on the **Karate Chop point**, I again say: "Even though I felt so hurt when Mom criticized me for not winning first place, I deeply and completely love and accept myself."

Then I begin tapping the **Eye Brow** point for seven to ten taps while I say: "Feeling so hurt when Mom criticized me for not winning first place."

Then I move to the **Side of the Eye** point and tap for seven to ten taps while I say: "Feeling so hurt when Mom criticized me for not winning first place."

Then I move to the **Under Eye** point and tap for seven to ten taps while I say: "Feeling so hurt when Mom criticized me for not winning first place."

Then I move to the **Under Nose** point and tap for seven to ten taps while I say: "Feeling so hurt when Mom criticized me for not winning first place."

Then I move to the **Chin** point and tap for seven to ten taps while I say: "Feeling so hurt when Mom criticized me for not winning first place."

Then I move to the **Collarbone** point and tap for seven to ten taps while I say: "Feeling so hurt when Mom criticized me for not winning first place."

Then I move to the **Under Arm** point and tap for seven to ten taps while I say: "Feeling so hurt when Mom criticized me for not winning first place."

Then I move to the **Top of the Head** point and tap for seven to ten taps while I say: "Feeling so hurt when Mom criticized me for not winning first place."

Then I stop tapping, take a deep breath in through my nose, and release it through my mouth. I have a sip of water and check in on how I feel. I do a new rating of how hurt the memory feels.

Let's say it's now down to a 7 and I want to keep working on this issue.

So now, because I'm working on the same issue, I will use the "remaining issue set-up."

The tapping round will go like this:

# Remaining Issue Set-Up

Tapping on the **Karate Chop point** I say: "Even though **I still have some of this** hurt feeling from when Mom criticized me for not winning first place, I deeply and completely love and accept myself."

Still tapping on the **Karate Chop point,** I again say: "Even though **I still have some of this** hurt feeling from when Mom criticized me for not winning first place, I deeply and completely love and accept myself."

A third time while still tapping on the **Karate Chop point,** I again say: "Even though **I still have some of this** hurt feeling from when Mom criticized me for not winning first place, I deeply and completely love and accept myself."

Then I begin tapping the **Eye Brow** point for seven to ten taps while I say: "**This remaining hurt feeling** from when Mom criticized me for not winning first place."

Then I move to the **Side of the Eye** point and tap for seven to ten taps while I say: "**This remaining hurt feeling** from when Mom criticized me for not winning first place."

Then I move to the **Under Eye** point and tap for seven to ten taps while I say: "**This remaining hurt feeling** from when Mom criticized me for not winning first place."

Then I move to the **Under Nose** point and tap for seven to ten taps while I say: "**This remaining hurt feeling** from when Mom criticized me for not winning first place."

Then I move to the **Chin** point and tap for seven to ten taps while I say: "**This remaining hurt feeling** from when Mom criticized me for not winning first place."

Then I move to the **Collarbone** point and tap for seven to ten taps while I say: "**This remaining hurt feeling** from when Mom criticized me for not winning first place."

Then I move to the **Under Arm** point and tap for seven to ten taps while I say: "**This remaining hurt feeling** from when Mom criticized me for not winning first place."

Then I move to the **Top of the Head** point and tap for seven to ten taps while I say: "**This remaining hurt feeling** from when Mom criticized me for not winning first place."

Then I stop tapping, take a deep breath in through my nose, and release it through my mouth. I have a sip of water and check in on how I feel.

Perhaps I note in my journal other feelings coming up for tapping on.

Then I re-rate the intensity. If it's not down to a 0, I can continue using the same "remaining feeling" sequence I've just done until it's down to a 0.

If it's at a 0, I will test. I'll do everything possible to get it to come back up and get myself feeling hurt in that memory again. If I jotted down a new aspect about that memory, I do the same procedure with this new feeling.

If I can't get it to come back up, the chances are very good that that blockage is now cleared permanently and, no matter when I think of that memory, it will not produce that feeling of hurt, and I'm far less likely to be triggered in the present moment by experiences that remind my subconscious of that memory. This file has now been updated, and the energy blockage released.

This point is key. Just as our current reality is a reflection of our beliefs, the things that upset us or cause intense emotional reactions are usually a hint of unresolved blockages. By clearing the original (or earliest) painful memories, it shows up as a release of the present-day discomfort. For example, a present-day fear of flying can be eliminated by clearing the emotional charge from the old memories that caused the blockage.

You'll find that with persistence you can make great progress continuing with EFT on your own following this basic process. Re-reading your earliest journal entries (and looking at the ratings you've noted) will show you just how far you've come.

You'll be amazed at how different you start to feel. Things just won't seem to bother you like they once did. You'll likely even have a sense of "feeling lighter" and more joyful as you go about your days.

At any time if you find that there's something you're not able to fully release on your own, or if there's a complex issue that you'd like some guided support with, again, please consider working with a trained practitioner.

Remember: Your sub-conscious is trying to protect you, so it can be very good at hanging on to past habits and patterns, even though you now consciously want to let them go. Working together with a practitioner, you'll be able to find what's "hiding from you," and you'll have the support you need to gently release even the most intense issues.

## Turn and Face Your Fears—Then Tap the Crap Outta Them!

One of my favorite starting points to suggest to people so they can quickly see what they are capable of when using EFT on their own, as well as get a jump-start on letting go of what's holding them back, is an exercise I call Timeline Tapping.

Timeline Tapping is a powerful exercise based on the Personal Peace Procedure that was posted on Gary Craig's original EFT website. The idea is to list all the painful memories you can think of and then systematically "tap the crap out of them." Essentially, you jump in with both feet *and* still go at your own pace to bring about a profound shift within yourself that gently unfolds over the course of a few months.

To get started, grab your journal and turn to a blank page. At the top of the page, and at the top of the next few pages, write the following headers (one per page): Age 0-10; Age 11-20; Age 21-30; Age 31-40; Age 41-50; and continue on in 10 year increments until you reach the decade containing your current age.

Once the page headers are done, spend some time recalling all the painful and upsetting experiences you've had and jot them down on the appropriate page based on your age when they took place. Just use a few words to capture the feeling and the experience. We'll be creating movie titles for the items on your list so that's the gist of the format to use.

I typically suggest starting with the biggest ones that immediately come to mind, flipping back and forth between the various pages to list them. Once the "easy-to-remember" ones are listed, go a bit deeper by spending some time contemplating each decade looking for more. Most people will come up with one to two dozen memories for each decade. But don't worry if it doesn't flow at first; just stick with it and things will come. If while doing this you recall certain memories that once really upset you, but don't seem as upsetting now, jot them down anyway. The fact that they came to you while doing this exercise suggests a need for resolution.

This part of the exercise can be spread out over a few days, and you can even continue to add to your lists as more memories surface while you're doing the next step.

A couple of examples are:

**Age 0-10:**

- Frightened when Dad shouted at me that time in the car when he almost crashed.
- Totally embarrassed when my fifth-grade class laughed at me when I gave my dolphin speech.

**Age 31-40:**

- Outraged by that disrespectful e-mail from Rachel about the new account—who does she think she is!
- So hurt that Dave didn't even thank me for making him look good with the great job I did on that presentation.

When you feel your list is complete, the next step is to begin the systematic tapping. This sounds intense but all it is is selecting one or more items *every day* and spending a few minutes tapping the intensity of the emotion off the memory using basic EFT.

So on the first day, you scan through your lists and decide where to tap. Maybe something immediately comes to you, and you feel that's the place to start. Or maybe, you decide you'll work on one decade at a time. However you decide to go about it is just perfect. There are no major rules other than to start and keep going every day.

Once you select a memory, spend a moment and get in touch with it to give it a rating using our 0-10 scale. Do any modifications to your note to create a movie title for the memory, including the feeling and a few words describing it. Then begin tapping as you did earlier using basic EFT.

At the end of the round, take a big breath in through your nose and exhale through your mouth, and check in. How are you feeling about the memory? What's the rating on it now? Be certain to notice any aspects that come up and treat them as separate events. (Add them to the list with their own "movie title" and rating, and apply EFT to them as well.)

Continue tapping through each event until you either laugh about it (it happens!) or you can't think about it anymore with any intensity even if you try to get upset over it. This is when you can call it resolved and move on to the next one.

If you get the intensity lowered but not to 0, assume something is hiding from you, and apply several full rounds of EFT on it from every angle you can think of for the highest possibility of resolving it completely.

Apply EFT to one or even a few items on your list every day until your list is completely tapped out. By systematically tapping on just a few memories each day, you'll feel a profound shift happen within you.

Be sure to pause and reflect as you go about this project.

Notice how your body feels better. Notice how your overall threshold for getting upset has dramatically improved. Notice how you begin to see things (and people) differently. Notice the improvement in your relationships.

And notice what it feels like to experience more peace in your life no matter what is going on. By doing this exercise alone, you can transform your life even if you don't make any other adjustments.

> *Peace – It does not mean to be in a place where there is no noise, trouble or hard work. It means to be in the midst of those things and still be calm in your heart.*
>
> ~ Author unknown

## Meridian Tapping Techniques (MTT)

I tend to use EFT as my primary tapping method when tapping to release the pain from past experiences. Most excessive negative emotional occurrences showing up today can usually be traced back to events that happened in the past. When I'm first starting out with a client, we clear as many past pains as possible, starting from the ones as far back as possible. I do this because the older memories (as in the ones closest to childhood) are often more relevant than the later ones. As mentioned before, our beliefs are mostly in place by age 7, and the events after that are merely the evidence we gather to support the belief. So by going back as far as possible, you'll likely get more healing bang for your tapping buck.

Then, once the "biggies" from the past are handled, I love to switch over to a variety of other tapping techniques that all fall under the general category of Meridian Tapping Techniques, or MTT for short.

MTT is the umbrella term used to describe a variety of energy healing techniques that all get results by tapping on the meridians to release blockages. Dr. Patricia Carrington created a tapping method called the Choices Method, and since then there are virtually as many tapping variations as there are practitioners.

I love the freedom in these "free-flow styles," and I use them primarily for tapping in new experiences. It's with the intention of bringing about or "tapping in" new ways of being that I highly recommend you give them a try. Please note, though, that I do not suggest using these styles for releasing past pain or trauma.

However, one area I find that lends itself very well to a general variation of EFT is tapping on limiting beliefs. Remember those beliefs we surfaced up and identified in Chapter 3? This is where they come into play.

I categorize tapping on beliefs more suitable for MTT tapping because we aren't exactly going to rate the discomfort of the belief, because our beliefs or truths likely aren't painful. But we do want to rate them so we can measure our progress at tapping, so for beliefs tapping we measure how true they are for us.

For example, if after doing the beliefs exercises you noticed a pattern where a number of your beliefs could all fall under the category of "change is scary," you could try running this through this process.

You identify the belief you would like to work on and you rate it on a scale of 0–10 for how true it is (0 being not true and 10 being 100 percent true), and you can likely get a feel for this right in your gut when you say it. NOTE: If, when you say any of these belief statements, any painful memories come to you that have an emotional charge, you will want to do basic EFT on these painful memories first and then come back to the beliefs tapping.

Sometimes we have a belief that only feels partially true for us. In this case the rating can be used to rate a percentage of truth we feel. I like to mention this "percentage of truth" for the rating up front because as you do this work in general, and this beliefs tapping in particular, a funny thing will likely happen. You'll likely begin to feel yourself letting go of the belief even as you're tapping.

For example, when you first say "change is scary" you could feel a tightening in your stomach area and know within you that that is true for you, 100 percent. After doing a few rounds of tapping, when you say "change is scary" part of you believes it but part of you starts noticing evidence that supports that sometimes it's not. You don't fully believe that change is not scary yet, but there is a little voice inside starting to let you know about times when it wasn't. When you look at the current events (and past events) of your life, you begin seeing the examples of how there have been times when making changes wasn't scary and, in fact, even examples of times when it's been downright fun. Some of the beliefs you've already identified may even be in this "yes, it is/no, it's not" 100-percent true state, and this tapping will work well with those, too.

To begin, identify the belief you have and its percentage of truth rating, and even jot down some "real-life proof" you have supporting your belief. Have some water handy, and you're all set to do a few rounds of beliefs tapping.

It's the same basic idea as we did before where we do the set-up three times, but as you tap through the points you can have some freedom with this tapping. It's more of a free-flow, conversational-style tapping where you can say the belief and tap, and also recite some of the proof you have while you tap, and you can say the part of you that doesn't believe it.

The other freedom is that with all this free-flow, conversation-with-yourself-style tapping, you just keep going until you feel it's done. You don't need to stop after one round; you just carry on and keep tapping the points, seven to ten times each, while talking about your belief out loud. Three to five full rounds before you stop and re-rate is perfectly normal for this.

So a quick example to show you might go like this:

Belief:  Change is scary.

Truth rating:  9/10

Set-up three times while tapping on the KC point

Even though I have this pretty big belief that change is scary, I deeply and completely love and accept myself.

After doing the set-up three times, you move on to tapping through the points over and over again until you feel like stopping.

EB:  Change is scary.

SE:  Change is scary and I have a ton of proof.

UE:  Change is scary because there's so much I can't control.

UN:  Change is scary.

CH:  Change has always been scary.

CB:  Change is scary.

UA:  Change is scary because I can't predict what will happen.

TH:  And I don't know if I can handle new things.

EB: Change is scary.
SE: I'm afraid of not knowing so change is scary.
UE: Change is scary. Everyone says so.
UN: And they know change is scary.
CH: And I know change is scary. Everyone knows.
CB: Change is scary. Better to avoid it.
UA: Overall, change is scary.
TH: But sometimes it's not.
EB: But mostly it's scary.
SE: Sometimes it's exciting.
UE: But mostly change is scary.
UN: And I don't like scary changes.
CH: But come to think of it, that last job change was the best thing that ever happened.
CB: But change is scary.
UA: But what if it didn't have to be?
TH: What if change could be like an adventure?
EB: I like adventures.
SE: Change is like an adventure.
UE: But change is scary.
UN: No, it's not. It's exciting.
CH: Change is exciting.
CB: Change is exciting, damn it!
UA: Because why wouldn't it be?
TH: Change is an adventure.
EB: There has been some proof but I didn't believe it.
SE: But that was just because I was looking at it differently.

UE: Now I know change is exciting like an adventure to a new land.

UN: But part of me doesn't totally believe it.

CH: Part of me is still scared that change is scary.

CB: But part of me is willing to try on the idea that change doesn't have to be scary anymore.

UA: And if part of me is ready.

TH: The rest of me will follow me on my "enjoying change" adventure!

On and on it will go. I love this style of tapping and often call it "Parts of the Self" tapping. It's when a part of you believes one thing and a part of you doesn't, and it's like having the two parts of yourself talk it out—all while tapping. I've had clients do this style of tapping with beliefs they've held onto as *the* absolute truth. They start out in disbelief that tapping this way will help, but after tapping for a bit they begin smiling and even end up bursting out laughing as the belief is released.

This tapping style, unlike the tapping for clearing past pain, can be very lighthearted and fun. I actually encourage you to allow this to be as much fun as possible.

The idea of allowing brings me back to Dr. Patricia Carrington's Choices Method.

The basic idea behind the Choices Method was to end the set-up with a more positive choice rather than the EFT standard affirmation of "I deeply and completely love and accept myself."

I love the idea of the Choices Method and have combined it with a couple of other methods and use them collectively as choosing, permission, and allowing tapping.

This type of tapping works so well with the Law of Attraction.

Remember in the Law of Attraction we established that the idea was, in every moment, to send the most "feel good" signal as possible to the Universe for matching. We talked about doing this temporarily with the breaking-state habits.

We've also established the whole point of EFT is to release the pain from past events so that this pain (or fear, or sadness, or anxiety, or any other of the "misery door" signals) is not running in the background, because all our present-day experiences are filtered through them, even though we try to pretend they're not. Because it's our true feelings that are being sent out to the Universe to match.

So, we use an energy healing or energy management tool like EFT to balance our feelings about past events so that they are cleared and we feel better, resulting is us sending a "happier" signal to be matched.

We talked about the idea that often current-day events are just reminding us of the original pain we experienced (this is also called "triggering"—as in, a current event is triggering an unresolved negative emotion from the past), so the farther back we can go in our memories to release the pain from the past the better, because this will stop current events from triggering negative feelings in us.

Once we've released all this pain, which has in some cases been the only way we know how to experience things, then what? Well, one idea to figure this out is to be open to allowing in more of the things behind that "bliss door"—to choose them for our life and then give ourselves permission to experience them.

You see, it's like that elephant again. We've lived by our beliefs for as many years as we've lived, so if we, all of a sudden, attempt to do things completely differently without showing the subconscious that it's a safe, gonna-be-good-so-we-should-do-more-of-it idea, it won't allow it. It may take one step but will very quickly get us back into our old patterns at even the slightest sign of discomfort with the new approach.

With this style of tapping, we paint a picture of how great the new "way" will be. It's like dangling a bucket of peanuts out in front of the elephant: showing him what to expect by trying this, and we tap it in to give the elephant a reason to step in the direction we want him to. This gives the subconscious a reason to incorporate new routines, beliefs, and habits in place of the ones we're releasing or updating.

It goes something like this. You think about something in your current reality that is not how you want it. Again, you can flip back to the first chapter and have a look at your Happiness/Success ratings for these, and try it on something tangible and real to you.

Perhaps it was in the area of finances where you're really struggling.

So we'll call this struggling financially.

Next you jot down or "capture" any thoughts and feelings that you have about this. Again, if this surfaces any uncomfortable memories, go back and do EFT on them before moving forward.

Then, just like we did in the Law of Attraction "Stop and Switch" exercise, jot down what the most amazing experience you would like to be having instead of the current troublesome experience would be. Make it super-duper amazing. Perhaps you come up with "total financial freedom so that I'm set for life financially."

To help you get to the super-duper, best outcome possible, after you jot something down, see if you can make it better when you ask, "And then what?" When you're at the best outcome you likely won't be able to top it with another "and then what?" answer.

Then begin tapping on this at the Eyebrow point as you repeat the phrase "I am experiencing total financial freedom and I'm set for life." (Yes, skip the Karate Chop point for this.) Just tap from the Eye Brow, going through all the points and stopping to jot down all the things that come to your mind in opposition to this desired outcome statement

These are the "yeah buts" you have (or "tail enders," as Gary Craig calls them). They are all the reasons that come to you why this is simply not possible or not an option for you. These, again, are the beliefs you have for why the subconscious won't accept this as an option or allow it to happen. These are the keys to why you are stuck.

Once you've jotted these down, run them through the previous belief tapping (and/or through EFT if there are past memories with painful/uncomfortable emotion coming up as well).

Then, once you can say the best possible outcome statement without any internal resistance (those "yeah buts" are all gone) then you're ready to write down what you now give yourself permission to experience (or choose to experience) and what you allow into your life.

Perhaps you write: "I give myself permission to feel completely at peace around money knowing I will always have more than I need."

And perhaps you come up with an allowing statement such as: "I allow financial freedom to come to me through means I've never even thought of before."

It's important to note here that when creating your choosing/permission/allowing statements that you don't reference from where you are in the present moment (e.g., "I want to earn more money so I'm not living paycheck to paycheck.") but instead, that you're going for the best possible outcome focusing only on what you do want.

Once you have these statements identified, you're ready to do this fun three-part round of tapping, which goes as follows:

Do the first set-up three times while tapping on the Karate Chop point.

KC: "Even though I'm struggling financially, I deeply and completely love and accept myself."

Then you tap each of the points seven to ten times while repeating the negative statement

EB: "I'm struggling financially."

SE: "I'm struggling financially."

UE: "I'm struggling financially."

UN: "I'm struggling financially."

CH: "I'm struggling financially."

CB: "I'm struggling financially."

UA: "I'm struggling financially."

TH: "I'm struggling financially."

For the second round you again do a set-up three times with the following wording:

"Even though I'm struggling financially, I give myself permission to feel completely at peace around money, knowing I will always have more than I need."

You then tap each of the points, stating the permission statement.

EB: "I give myself permission to feel completely at peace around money, knowing I will always have more than I need."

SE: "I give myself permission to feel completely at peace around money, knowing I will always have more than I need."

UE: "I give myself permission to feel completely at peace around money, knowing I will always have more than I need."

UN: "I give myself permission to feel completely at peace around money, knowing I will always have more than I need."

CH: "I give myself permission to feel completely at peace around money, knowing I will always have more than I need."

CB: "I give myself permission to feel completely at peace around money, knowing I will always have more than I need."

UA: "I give myself permission to feel completely at peace around money, knowing I will always have more than I need."

TH: "I give myself permission to feel completely at peace around money, knowing I will always have more than I need."

Then for the third round, you do the set up again three times with the following wording:

"Even though I'm struggling financially, I allow financial freedom to come to me through means I've never even thought of before."

You then tap each of the points, stating the allowing statement.

EB: "I allow financial freedom to come to me through means I've never even thought of before."

SE: "I allow financial freedom to come to me through means I've never even thought of before."

UE: "I allow financial freedom to come to me through means I've never even thought of before."

UN: "I allow financial freedom to come to me through means I've never even thought of before."

CH: "I allow financial freedom to come to me through means I've never even thought of before."

CB: "I allow financial freedom to come to me through means I've never even thought of before."

UA: "I allow financial freedom to come to me through means I've never even thought of before."

TH: "I allow financial freedom to come to me through means I've never even thought of before."

After you complete this, take a moment to write in your journal. Record what you feel and where your thoughts lead you. Take note of any inspired ideas that come to you as well, because these are very important.

As you clear away the limiting beliefs and thoughts, you get in touch with the naturally resourceful and creative side of yourself. Inspirations and new ideas begin to flow from you.

With a little practice, you will likely find that this becomes a favorite tapping routine, because this style of tapping can result in mind-blowing ideas and synchronicities. So be sure to have fun and journal about what's taking place.

To create even more mind-blowing results, try this next idea.

# Chapter
# 6

## Visualization...With a Twist!

## Visualization...With a Twist!

Visualization has been around forever. As a matter of fact, it's another one of those highly effective systems we humans come equipped with right from the get-go.

In our earliest days, it shows up as none other than our imagination. As anyone who's ever witnessed young children amusing themselves for hours, if not days, with a large cardboard box can attest to, imagination is a pretty cool thing to behold. But then, as we travel along on our journey to becoming mature, serious adults, the next label we commonly apply to visualization is daydreaming. In addition to the name change, the concept of spending time making pictures in your mind's eye also takes on a bit of a negative connotation, as in "Are you sitting daydreaming again? Why don't you get up and do something worthwhile?"

While this is unfortunate, it's not as bad as what takes place next. You see, probably the most blasphemous type of visualization that we humans have come up with can be seen taking place every day by grown adults everywhere. Worse than just it happening is that it's almost revered as being a good thing to do, as if it somehow improves things that aren't working out so well. Its name, you wonder? This insidious form of visualization goes by none other than worry. Yep, worry!

For many, worry has become the adult version of imagination. But rather than being the delightful and playful way to fill our thoughts with wonder and happiness that we enjoyed so much as children, over the years it turns into a much darker form of visualization. But it is equally powerful.

If you're wondering why worry is so negative and something you're probably going to want to discontinue doing, it's this: Remember the Universe's job? Matching 365/24/7, right? When you worry, your thoughts and feelings in the present moment are all about fretting and stressing over future events. Even though the events are in the future, and not definitely going to happen, it is in the present moment that you are feeling all the worry and stressful feelings. So in the present moment, what signal do you think you're sending out to the Universe to match?

Yep, the signal you're sending to be matched is the stressful worrisome feelings you're having. So the Universe gets your signal, and it doesn't interpret that this isn't a real situation, nor does it interpret that it's an event off in the future. Nope, its only job is to match the signal it's getting right now, so it will match your current worrisome stressful feeling signal and send back more situations so feel the same way about.

In case you didn't quite catch that, let me say it again: When you worry about awful possibilities for the future, in that very moment you send a "worrisome, awful, stressful" signal for matching, and therefore you are inviting more "feel bad, misery door" people, places, and things into your life. So, just by sitting worrying over the current "feel bad, misery door" people, places, and things that are already in your life (or even that are in someone else's life when it's someone else you're worrying about!) you're essentially requesting more to feel exactly the same about. Worry and stress are truly like double-edged swords.

If that weren't reason enough to jump ship on worrying, how about this: In any given situation that you are worrying about, there is absolutely no way for you to know if it's going to turn out as bad as you are "worrying" about. However, by spending your present moment being in misery and worrying about what might happen, you are guaranteeing that you get to feel bad about it at least once. You're sitting there worrying, stressing, and feeling awful in your present moment, thinking about something that's not even happening. So you're choosing a perfectly good "now" moment to feel awful just by thinking what you are thinking.

And lastly, and this might seem even more of an "in your face" point, but the naked truth is this: No matter how bad you feel about something, you can't possibly feel bad enough (or worry enough) about it to make it better.

That's right. No matter how bad you make yourself feel thinking about it, it won't make the situation better. As they say, worrying and stressing about something is nothing more than the illusion that you're doing something constructive to help the problem.

So if you've ever worried about something, or found yourself saying "I'm worried sick," take heart. The good news is that your ability to visualize is in top form. Now is your chance to use your visualization powers for good.

# Visualization...With a Twist!

As usual, before I go into the "how to" on this, I want to tell you a little more about why you might like to get on board and try this.

You see, the thing is, our minds don't know if something is real or imagined. This is why, to varying degrees, people will cry at sad movies or be scared senseless at scary ones. Lots of research has been done in this area. In fact, in one such test, test subjects were hooked up to all sorts of measuring electrodes to record their nervous system changes and muscle reactions as these test subjects were visualizing themselves jogging. They actually weren't jogging at all but were visualizing that they were. Sure enough, during the visualization the test equipment registered as if they were physically jogging.

Additional studies have reported that in physical training versus visualized training, both sets of test subjects were equally prepared physically for the activities. That is, the test subjects who visualized themselves training were as prepared physically as the ones who actually did the physical training.

Further studies have gone on to show that this holds true for all visualized behaviors and activities, not just for athletic performance. Ultimately our bodies believe that what we visualize has already occurred or is currently occurring.

At the risk of going too science-y here, what's even more interesting is that, when you visualize something, your body is creating a memory of the visualization you're practicing. So just as practicing something physically results in it becoming easier as we practice it over and over again, the same increase in efficiency occurs just by visualizing we're practicing it over and over again.

Just like taking a shortcut over a grassy lawn on a regular basis will result in a path being created as the grass is worn away, the same thing happens here: The repeated visualization will "create a path" for us, and, because our bodies are creatures of habit, when given a choice, they will more likely than not choose the positive visualization "path" option if and when the scenario presents itself in real life. In other words, your body/mind will go for the path that's already created when your reality appears to match what you've visualized, because it's more familiar with that than charting new territory, even if the path was created in your imagination!

For example (and for simplicity, let's stick with a physical example here), suppose you are scheduled to run a marathon. As part of your training, you spend time visualizing all aspects of the race and the experiences you want to have, from your training and prep for the race, right through to your arrival and all the congratulations you will experience at the finish line. You visualize it all in great detail. Come race day, your body is more likely to attempt to duplicate that which it believes it's already experienced over and over again than to reach for a new option. In other words, it will attempt to duplicate that which you've visualized. So the more details you visualize that you want, the more your mind will attempt to duplicate. When you add emotion into this mix, it's like a supercharger.

Another reason why visualization is so powerful (and yes, this is a wee bit science-y, too) is due to a tiny part of the brain called the Reticular Activating System, or RAS.

The RAS also has a matching function. It's basically the part of the brain responsible for sorting through the billions of bits of information you are exposed to every day. It sorts the info and highlights the pieces that are a match to what you are interested in. You see, because we are exposed to so much information and because our brains can't possibly process it all, some of it just passes us by without it registering. The RAS is responsible for flagging the things we are interested in and having them stand out from all the other bits that we're not interested in.

For example, have you ever become interested in purchasing something—say a new car? After you start getting interested in a particular car, it seems that they're *everywhere*. This doesn't happen because all of a sudden there's been an increase in supply now that you want one; it's simply that this car is now showing up in your RAS as important to you, so your RAS alerts you to all the occurrences of it that are around. Before it was of interest to you—that is, before you sent the signal to the RAS that it mattered—these items just flowed by without hitting your radar or you noticing them.

Just like in our Hot and Cold game, if the things you are looking to be, do, and have in your life are actually right there in plain sight, practicing visualization is a surefire way to have you begin to see them.

One last reason for visualizing is simply this: If you are sending signals for the Universe to match and respond to by sending you back people, places, and things that you'll get to feel the exact same way about, which signal would you rather send and receive more of: the "misery door" signal by thinking worrisome thoughts, or the "bliss door" signal by visualizing experiencing the very things you do want? In any given moment, you—and only you—have dominion over your thoughts and the thoughts you think will influence what you feel. This is what your signal to the Universe is all about.

*Thoughts become things…choose the good ones.*
~ Mike Dooley

## Add a Twist

That's some information about what visualization can do as well as a pretty compelling case as to why you might like to give it a try; and this brings me to the twist part.

Vision boards have become a favorite tool of many folks wanting to get connected to the things they want in their life. These are collections of pictures and affirmations put together collage-style and placed in a prominent location to remind you of the things you want to be, do, or have in your life.

While they work for some, I've also heard from clients who have them but aren't really inspired by them. Descriptions range from mild interest to total indifference. So if you have created a vision board that's just not doing it for you, this might help.

The drawback to looking up at a collage of pictures alone is that it's comparable to looking at one poster to get a feel for a movie. It's a static, two-dimensional image that can lose your attention after a while, and thereby not inspire you.

Sometimes vision boards even have the reverse effect to inspiration. Occasionally, after the initial delight over the creation wears off, looking at it begins to trigger negative thoughts and feelings—as in, "Yeah, right. As if I'll have that." So if you are currently using a vision board and at times find yourself feeling negative about it, the good news is that it's doing a good job; it's just not quite the job you intended.

You see, if you look at your vision board and are coming up with negative thoughts and feelings, it's actually surfacing up your limiting beliefs and blockages about what you want to have in your life. Grab your journal and try jotting down what your real feelings are, and do some belief tapping on them. And then try visualizing with a twist!

My version of inspirational visualizing with a twist can be used instead of, or in addition to, your static photo collage. For this, I'm suggesting you get back in touch with that imagination of yours, and I'm even suggesting that you dare go so far as to do a little daydreaming!

Yep, you read that right. The idea is to do like those test-subject athletes did. Make a movie in your mind of what you would like to be experiencing in your dream life. See the whole shebang unfolding in your mind's eye, starting with the end result—as in, start as if what you want has already occurred. And don't just see it, involve as many senses as you can and get your feelings and emotions involved, too.

To simplify this I've come up with seven steps to visualizing with a twist.

The seven steps are:

1. **Write it in your journal.** Write your dream-visions in a journal so you can read them often. Use first-person present tense ("I am") statements, writing as if it's already your current reality and not something off in the future that you're wanting. Write with conviction and a knowing that it's already your experience. Don't pay to much attention to the physical details of the things or people, and definitely don't attempt to come up with the "how" to make it happen. Your job with this journal writing is to define the experience you're going for. Define the what (the experience) and the whys (again, the experience and feelings you expect to get from the things you say you want).

    Whenever you can, also incorporate joyful experiences and characteristics you've already known into your new visions. For example, to amplify and anchor the feeling of being appreciated, I once wrote, "I feel so appreciated here, just like that time when I got that unexpected 'good attitude and job well done bonus.'" You can do the same with characteristics of people, places, and things that have brought you joy. Take the best of the best of what you've already experienced, and add it to your "composite" for the new experience.

2. **Anchor by adding uplifting, upbeat music.** "Anchoring" means to link two things together—as in, one thing happens and it automatically brings the other to mind. One way to bring about joyful feelings is by listening to your favorite songs. Just as this is one of the breaking-state exercises for lifting your spirits, we bring it in here also to get the feelings soaring as you're dreaming up your phenomenal life. You can even assign specific songs to specific visualizations. Play your favorite music while writing and reading over what you've written in your journal. This is a double whammy for sending out a "bliss door" signal for the Universe to match! Another plus to anchoring your phenomenal life visualizations to your favorite music is that, after doing this a few times, whenever you hear the songs you've used in your visualizations, no matter where you are, the songs will remind you of your visualized "dream life" thoughts.

3. **Imagine your dreams as being your reality right now.** After you've written about them in journal (or re-read them), bring the ideas to life by making moving pictures of your wonderful reality right there in your imagination. This can feel awkward at first, particularly if you're holding negative associations to daydreaming. (And at the risk of sounding repetitive, do some tapping if this is the case.) Some different ways to experience these movies of your mind are to first perhaps watch the movie as if it's out in front of you, like it's a movie of you projected on a screen. Then after you're comfortable with this, try zooming in on it so it's bigger and closer. Finally, when you've mastered visualizing that way, try pausing the movie and imagine you're stepping into the scene. From this perspective, you're no longer watching yourself in the movie out in front of you, but you're actually in it, taking part in all the activity. From there, visualize yourself immersed in your wonderful dream life as often as you can.

4. **Include as many of your senses in your visualizations as you can.** Make a point of noticing not just the sights but the textures, the sounds, the smells, and even the tastes.

5. **Add as many emotions and internal feelings as you can.** Visualize

yourself feeling exactly what it is you know you would be feeling if this were your reality, and immerse yourself in these feelings as if you've already achieved what you want.

6. **Feel the appreciation and gratitude that you'll feel when your visualized reality is your present-day reality.** In other words, if you were now experiencing all the things you want to be, do, and have, how appreciative and grateful are you feeling about it? Feel this as part of your visualizations.

7. **The biggest twist of all is to tap on your EFT/MTT points the entire time you visualize!** Yep, the entire time you're marinating in your dream life in your thoughts, tap about seven to ten times on each of your tapping points.

To give you an example of what this process might look like, suppose you want to visualize your dream job.

Start by writing about you vision for your dream life in your journal. This can be an ongoing entry that you build upon as new ideas come to you. Perhaps in one entry you write about waking up each day feeling inspired and eager to get to work. Perhaps you write about being surrounded by friendly co-workers and a boss who not only appreciates your contribution but lets you know this on a regular basis. Perhaps you write about a tremendous feeling of accomplishment at doing a job you love and doing it well.

The job description details are not important with this, because ultimately, when it comes right down to it, most of us are really seeking the experiences that we think the people, places, and things, and, in this example, a new job, will provide.

This feeling experience can come to us from a number of ways—even from ones we haven't even thought of, so when you focus on the feeling experience, it's like ordering off the full menu rather than just having access to the familiar, shortened "daily specials" menu. The Universe is always conspiring on our behalf for our highest good, so by leaving the details of the exact fit to the Universe, and concentrating on sending a laser-focused signal about the feelings we want to have, it's as if magic occurs. People, places, and opportunities appear, as if out of nowhere, at exactly the right time.

The next step is the music. Have it playing (I prefer loud whenever possible, but go with your personal preference) as you're writing in your journal about your vision as well as when you're reading over it. In this example, you put on your favorite song. Maybe it relates to work or is a song you like listening to while you're working, or maybe it's completely unrelated but you just *love* it.

The music is playing (on repeat if possible, or have a few songs queued up). You've written and read over the items in your journal and are feeling really good. Then, either with eyes open or closed, begin visualizing that you're already at your ideal job, just as you've described it in your journal.

Create movies in your mind's eye of the experience you're having at your dream job while you tap on your tapping points.

A visualization for your perfect job might be something like this: You're walking up to your place of work. You open the door and walk in, and the place is alive with energy. You feel yourself smile as you hear laughter coming from off in the distance. As you walk down the hall toward the coffee area, you notice the aromatic smell of a fresh pot of coffee brewing. You're greeted with smiles and cheery "good mornings." You enter the coffee area and, as always, it feels so welcoming and bright. It turns out it's the senior manager leading the laughter. A group of staff from various positions are all wrapping up a lively discussion as the coffee finishes brewing. It's slightly after starting time, but everyone here works at their own pace, so even if they get started a couple of minutes late, this is a place where that's OK.

You add a funny bit to the discussion, and everyone laughs. You always feel so connected here. You get your coffee and head to your office. Your boss motions you in as you pass his door and you say good morning. He thanks you for your input on the project you've been working on, telling you it was exactly what was needed and that he hadn't even thought of the option you presented. You walk out of his office feeling appreciated and inspired. This is a great place to work and you're *so* grateful it's where you work! You totally *love* this job!

That perhaps looked like it was a lot from the written version, but this little visualization would probably last less than a minute. It was the equivalent of having a sixty-second "bliss door" vacation right there when you wanted one. You can enjoy this mini-vacation of the mind whether you're stuck in a traffic jam (in which case your eyes would have been opened during the visualization☺!) or even if you're in a slow-moving line-up, or after a stressful encounter at your current job (in which case playing the music loud might not work out so well). Maybe you can't do the tapping in this situation, but the point is to do this dreaming as often as possible in place of the regular wandering thoughts you usually do have, and when you do dream include as many of the seven steps as you can.

I also want to point out that, in this example, you could be working for any number of companies and have any number of job responsibilities, but ultimately the feeling in the visualization is what's most important. This example gives a clear indication of the feelings; always when visualizing remember to immerse yourself in those feelings. Imagine them as your reality right now (not off in the future). See the scene over and over in your mind's eye and add to it. Every time you do this, feel the feelings, because these feelings (even though they're imagined) are the very feelings (signals) you're sending to the Universe in the present moment. So even if your little visualization break is taken in the midst of your current stressful job, by breaking the stressful state by doing the visualization, you're switching from sending a stressful "misery door" signal to sending a much more positive "bliss door" signal for the Universe to match.

The Universe, just like our minds, doesn't care if this is an imagined scene or something going on right now. The Universe doesn't interpret the scene, or tell time, or evaluate, or anything else. It only matches your signal so it can send back people, places, and things that match the signal it's receiving.

Also, your mind doesn't know that this vision isn't real. It doesn't need to; it simply goes about beginning to "carve it in" or imprint it so that, when given the choice, it will go to this as the default to match your reality to when the circumstances present themselves.

Your RAS is getting engaged to start finding you things that fill this bill. It's like a creative tension gap gets set up on all sides. How things are in your present reality is juxtaposed with how things are in your visualization, and the gap in between the two is like an over-stretched elastic pulling the two ends together—as in pulling your current reality toward your visualized reality and/or pulling your visualized reality toward your current reality.

The more intense you can get your feelings of joy, happiness, peace, excitement—all the great things you want to be feeling in your life—involved in the visualization, and the more senses you can involve, the more powerful this exercise becomes.

And remember to always, always connect to how grateful you are in the visualization, because gratitude and appreciation are like the magic that make it all happen.

> *Appreciation can make a day, even change a life. Your willingness to put it into words is all that is necessary.*
>
> ~ Margaret Cousins

# III

# Your Destination—Your Phenomenal Life: "From Now Often," Choosing, and Stepping Into It

*Contemplate yourself as surrounded by
the conditions you intend to produce.*
                              ~ Dr. Wayne Dyer

# Chapter 7

## Never Mind!

Way back in the late '70s, as a young teenager, I remember howling with laughter watching the comedy show *Saturday Night Live* and just loving when Roseanne Roseannadanna was on. If you're familiar with her, perhaps you're smiling now. If not, let me explain. Roseanne Roseannadanna was a character created by Gilda Radner. She was an explosive, crazy-haired, squeaky high-pitched voice anchorwoman brought on the "Weekend Update" news segments to give editorial replies to whatever the current issue was.

Only, the thing is that she always had things mixed up, ever so slightly but ever so monumentally. In one such mix-up, for example, Roseanne Roseannadanna was going on and on, with increasing passion in defense of violins on television. She stated her support of violins on television, and got more and more into her case. Then, just as she was getting into her zealous objection to violins only being shown at late hours because all viewers were entitled to good music by all instruments, and violins should not be segregated, the co-anchor leaned over and got Roseanne's attention to inform her that the topic was actually *violence* on television, not *violins* on television.

The scene ended, as they always did, with Roseanne Roseannadanna saying in her iconic squeaky, high-pitched voice, "Ohhhhh, that's very different. Never mind!"

I loved these skits then for the humor value, and to this day I love them because they illustrate so beautifully the idea of just accepting a new way of seeing something instantly when you get new information.

They show us how to set down our most compelling arguments with acceptance and even humor. If we've always done something one way, and now we have updated information that comes with the promise of producing the results we are looking for, imagine simply saying "Ohhhhh, that's very different. Never mind!

## Who Says? And What if They're Wrong?

This brings me to a very important point. We humans have adopted many rules for how things are. While these rules are designed to help things in our everyday lives go more smoothly as we collectively accept them, for the most part the rules are just a bunch of commonly accepted beliefs. And just like our individual beliefs, they're not always the truth.

Two such rules that I'd like to draw your attention to are: 1) Change is hard, and 2) Change must take a long time. You see, this simply isn't the truth. While it certainly can be, and perhaps you've even got a whole bunch of evidence supporting that this is true for you, I'll ask you to consider this: Who says it has to be, and what if they're wrong?

If this does ring true for you, and I bet you know where I'm going next, this is a tappable belief for you. There are loads of examples and stories about how change can happen in a flash and how it can be very easy. If you're up for tapping on these, I'm pretty sure you'll enjoy joining me in living to find proof to bust them.

I like to compare it to working on a file on a computer. Take a one-page Word document, for example. To change the document I simply click on the file, open the document, make my revision, and click save. The computer does its thing, and the document is saved. Suppose I then wanted to update a ten-page document. I would go through the same process: open the file, make my changes, and click save. Once again the computer would do its thing, and the larger document would be saved. It's not harder for the computer to save this bigger file, and it doesn't take any longer.

The same can be true for updating your belief files to bring about change in your life. It doesn't have to be hard, and it doesn't have to take a long time. This is totally up to you, depending on what you choose to believe.

I like to remind myself of this with my big, red "EASY" button I picked up at the local office supply store. There it sits on my desk, and, when I get all wrapped up in "making things hard," I reach out and pound on the button. A little recorded voice tells me "That was easy!" It's just a little state-breaking fun to remind me that I'm the only one making it so hard.

## Imperfect Really Means "I'm Perfect"!

Oftentimes we humans get so bogged down defending our views and beliefs and rules and ways of being that we lose the whole point. To refresh, the point is to feel good and have an amazing, joyful life in the present moment, and in so doing to send a "bliss door" signal up to the Universe to match and send us even more experiences to feel good about.

If, up until now, your life can't be described quite that way, and through reading these pages and doing the exercises you've begun to recognize that perhaps you're holding beliefs or practicing habits and having experiences that aren't producing the "bliss door," phenomenal-life sort of signals you'd like, then I invite you to try on simply accepting the notion that, in every moment of every day, you've been doing the best you can with the information you have. You no longer need to defend how you've been doing things, especially in the case of beliefs and patterns that are holding you back.

Consider instead that there are no mistakes and everything is right on schedule. Any experiences you've had that have "scarred or marred" you have created the individual you have become. As I implied with the heading, there are no imperfections. Imperfect is just a typo missing the apostrophe and a space. It is meant to be "I'm perfect." You, like everyone else! We are all doing our best with the information we have.

Now that you have new information, you can, in an instant, try on saying "Ohhhh, that's very different. Never mind!"

Imagine the freedom in simply letting go! Just like the fiery anchor-woman who was so passionately speaking on the subject, then, in an instant, with new information, she let it go.

## "From Now Often"

This is a quote from none other than my little Angel son, Tyler. At 5 ½ it's a lot of fun (and sometimes not!) to hear his take on phases and expressions he's heard and can say in context but not quite right—and even, as I've come to accept, the times when they're "righter" than I first realized.

"From now often" is Ty's way of saying "from now on, can we do this often?"—as in, "Momma, from now often, can I have three books at bedtime, please?"

I've stopped correcting him on this because I think it's rather catchy!

To help you tie in all of this information and bring it into to your life from now often, here's a recap of how to use the tools discussed, and a few more suggestions to assist you in letting go of what's no longer serving you.

## Noticing and Accepting

I talked about how many of us have employed the tactic of "pretending" or denying feelings and habits. This strategy can be the equivalent of putting frosting on a mud-pie: It may appear great from the outside to onlookers, and for a while you may even get away with it as fooling yourself, but eating such a concoction is not going to produce the experience you're hoping for. Neither does denying what's really there for you. *DENIAL,* after all, is an acronym for Don't Even Notice I Am Lying!

Instead, get real and honest, and dig in, because the first step to setting down limiting thoughts, beliefs, meanings, and habits is simply to become aware of them and accept them.

Use the beliefs and meaning exercises to get to those hidden and not-so-pretty places. Only you will know they're there, and you will be liberated simply by acknowledging them.

Also remember that your life—that is, your perceived reality, the people, places, and situations showing up in your life as your reality—is a mirrored reflection of your beliefs. If you believe life is hard, you will experience it this way.

Use your journal and the exercise pages from earlier to write about your "take" on life in general, and about your life in particular. From this identify what rules or beliefs you have for life and what they mean.

If you would like to adopt more empowering, updated beliefs, go back to Chapter 3 and review the meanings you've assigned to the events of your life. Then consider what new empowering meanings you could assign instead. For example, suppose between the ages of 31 and 40 you noted that you had a car crash and you assigned the meaning that life is filled with danger and you're not safe. What if you changed that meaning to "sometimes what's most important is right in front of me and I need to slow down (or stop) and look at it"? If this were the meaning you assigned, what new perspectives and views might emerge from looking at that same event with this meaning?

# Tapping

My favorite tool *ever* to release painful memories from the past and recurring negative reactions to present-day people, places, and situations is EFT.

EFT is an amazing, simple, fast, and effective tool that I encourage you to try on the big stuff and on the little stuff that is holding you back. My suggestion is to always use the basic EFT protocol for releasing past pain, remembering to go as far back in your memories as possible for the "bigger" ones.

For a more creative approach I recommend using the more general MTT, free-flow tapping. Try beliefs tapping when you still feel blocked but have used EFT on the specifics and now want to address the more general beliefs and *resistance* to moving forward.

As for how often to tap, tap whenever you feel like it, but aim for daily.

Part of being human in this big world is that we experience lots of people, places, and situations that cause negative emotional responses. Some are minor and some are major reflections of the very things that are blocking us.

So tap often to wipe the slate clean on what's holding you back, and then…

# Chapter
# 8

## Hold the Pickles

Another memory from my childhood was a commercial for some burger place announcing its new double burger. This particular commercial started with a catchy little jingle:

> *"Hold the pickles*
> *"Hold the lettuce*
> *"Special orders don't upset us*
> *"All we ask is that you let us*
> *"Serve it your way...*
> *"HAVE IT YOURRRRRRRR WAY...*
> *"It goes double now!"*

On and on the commercial went, with the whole point being that they were there to serve us up whatever we wanted—and, in double portions!

Once again, when I think of this now, I smile and think of it in terms of the Law of Attraction—as if it's the Universe singing directly to *me*, reminding me to send out signals of what I really really want—special orders and all! The Universe will then take care of filling my order and even doubling what I could have come up with for the specifics.

I bring this to your attention to emphasize that, if you want to begin really using the Law of Attraction, Tapping, and Visualization to create the life of your dreams, you need to first get clear about what that life looks like.

We used the earlier exercises to surface up your beliefs, habits, patterns, and disempowering meanings that are already there running in the background, and you'll use EFT and free-flow tapping on these.

If by chance you've noticed the apparent contradiction of focusing on the "pain" while doing EFT and are concerned that this will be sending a "misery door" signal out to the Universe while you do EFT, let me reassure you.

The "misery door" signal about the painful items you're going to apply EFT to is already being sent out, but it's not obvious because you've become so accustomed to it. Think of it like having your sunglasses perched on the top of your head; because you're so used to them being up there, you don't notice and end up searching for them when you want to wear them. You've been sending the signals out that are producing the results in your life, so if it's not as blissful as you'd like, know that the signals you're sending are behind the unsatisfactory results.

Also, EFT rounds are very fast, so even as we focus on the "misery door" signal for a few moments, the net result is that it's neutralized very quickly and the "misery door" signal is shut down. From there the energy flow is restored and the signal is improved! This not only sends an updated signal out in the present moment, but it also ensures that that "behind the scenes" signal that was sabotaging your efforts is dealt with—and usually permanently. Your new, lighter, "bliss door" thoughts and feelings can emerge, and from there that old elephant will stop going in his same-ol', same-ol' habitual directions and be open to your directions.

But that requires figuring out what you *do* want.

## Help Me Help You

Just as Tom Cruise said in the movie *Jerry Maguire,* the Universe is simply waiting for us to send the signal for what we really do want. And just like in that little jingle at the beginning of the chapter, special orders are "no problem."

This does present a slight problem when we send our signal by referencing all that we don't want, or if we're not specific about the "bliss door" items, or we focus mostly on the disappointing results we've seen so far. This sends out confusing or opposing signals, and the results can end up being even more disappointing.

And believe it or not, that's how many of us have been sending our signals for the life experiences we want: by referencing all that we don't want and/or by vaguely asking for more of the people, places, and things we do want—as in, "I want more money." Remember how I said the Universe is always conspiring on your behalf to fill your order? So if you've ever said that or thought that and ever found a penny on the ground, this would be the Universe providing for you that which you ask for. You wanted more money, and you got more money.

Now in case you're thinking, "Yeah, but that's not what I meant," remember that the Universe doesn't translate. Its only job is to match.

So in the moment you're saying "I want more money," you're probably referencing from looking at your current state of "I don't have enough money." Your signal to the Universe is one of fear and lack with a glimmer of hope, but mostly feelings of doubt. This is not exactly the "bliss door" sort of signal you were going for, but, when referencing from the lack you currently have, it's the conflicting signal you send. Off this signal goes to the Universe, and it gets matched with "more but not really more" and—ta da—you find a penny. You got more money!

It's not always that obvious and immediate, and I'll talk more about the timing aspect in a moment, but for now, are you starting to see my point about the importance of sending a crystal-clear, referencing-only-that-which-you-want, "bliss door" type signal?

But before you get scared that every single thought that crosses your mind is going to result in an immediate manifestation of "more of the same" showing up, it's not quite as immediate as that.

You see, your thoughts are governed by the same rules and beliefs that you hold, so it's like you have a collective theme going out. While you may have an "exception blip" type thought or feeling going out occasionally, the main signals that you're sending are from the thoughts and feelings you persistently immerse yourself in. For example, if you watch the news once and get caught up in the negativity of the day, but this is really in contrast to your patterned viewing habits or thoughts that the world is a loving place, then it's not a signal that's going out with much strength. If, however, you spend a great deal of time watching programs that upset you and then you persistently feel emotionally impacted and drained, then talk about the news and all the negative events, and hold thoughts that life is a struggle and you live in a ruthless dog-eat-dog world, then this is a prominent thought/feeling routine for you. This will reinforce the signal and thereby send out a stronger signal.

 This is why I suggest you add all the blissful emotions you expect to feel when you are visualizing because, by adding emotion to your thoughts, it's the equivalent of picking up a "hotline" to the Universe and putting the signal at the front of the line.

The things you routinely watch, the activities you persistently partake in, and even the words you persistently choose all affect your feelings and reinforce your beliefs, so this is one area that you might want consider having a closer look at to be sure you're getting really clear on ordering what you really want.

## Who Will I Be Without My Stuff?

The early days of clearing away our limiting beliefs and old pain and habits can feel both empowering and downright scary.

After all, we know what all that old painful stuff feels like. We know we can handle it; we know we can make it work and live with it. It may not be the best life, but it's tolerable. It may even be bad and it may be a lot of things, but it's usually all we've known, and, if we don't have the comfort of being immersed in our "stuff" who will we be? How will we navigate life?

We simply don't know who we are without our stuff.

When you start to clear away the blocks and patterns that you've always known, expect that at first it might feel a bit (or a lot) scary. Like a writer paralyzed by that first blank page, the initial fear of the unknown might have you consider running back to all that you've known, even if it is lousy. It's the old "devil you know versus the devil you don't" idea.

The best way to overcome this is to get really really clear on what you're heading toward so there is much less temptation to retreat to your unsatisfying, but known, comfort zone.

*Life begins as the edge of your comfort zone.*

~ Neale Donald Walsch

## Ordering!

A fun way I like to begin putting everything together after clearing away the past discomforts with tapping, and to get beyond the "just getting started paralysis," is on what I call my "Ordering!" form. Inspired by that little commercial jingle, I imagine that the Universe is like the staff of a restaurant all working together to get us our orders.

This sheet is based on this idea of ordering something simple like food, and it can be used for clarifying the details about the people, places, and things you want to experience in your life. Take a sheet of paper and divide it into four sections and label them as follows:

| I'd like... | Hold the... |
|---|---|
| Easy on the ... | And extra... |

If you think of ordering something at a restaurant, you often state what you want, then you enhance the basic order to make it even better. So you might have a preference and ask the waiter to bring you a veggie burger. (This is the basic order: "I'd like a _____.")

Then you begin to enhance the basic order by asking the waiter to modify it slightly to make it just as you like it, so you say, "Please hold the pickles." (Hold the things you don't want in your experience.) I often suggest you write these down first, because it will indicate if there is any emotional charge to clear with tapping, and second, because it often helps to clarify what you do want.

Then you might also ask the waiter to go a bit easy on something that usually comes with what you've ordered so you say, "Easy on the tomatoes." (State what you'd like some of, but maybe only a little.)

Lastly, you really enhance it by asking for extra of something you really like so you say, "And *extra* wasabi mayo, please." (Always ask for the extras that will take your experience from good to phenomenal!!!)

In the early days of defining what you would like and as a jumping-off point to get the ideas flowing for your visualization and journal work, this sheet is fun and easy to start with.

This form is also a great way to get clear about what you really do want. Imagine what your experience might be at a restaurant if you give your order to the waiter for that veggie burger. Then after a few minutes, you call him back and say you've changed your mind and that you'd like to have the nachos. He heads back to the kitchen. Then you see someone else being served something else that looks good, so you call the waiter over again and place yet another order. Finally, you're content with what you've ordered, but you notice that people who arrived much later than you are already finished their meal and getting their desserts. You start to wonder why your order isn't coming, and maybe you even begin to think that this is a lousy place to eat.

This again is an example of what happens when we're sending weak or conflicting signals up to the Universe. What we really want seems slow in coming, and we start to think that the process is lousy. Use this form to get clear on your order so you'll be sending up laser-focused signals for matching.

## No Man (or Woman) Is an Island

When you begin doing this work, you may also find that you begin feeling somewhat alone. I hear this a fair bit from clients, so I wanted to bring it up. Letting go of lifelong beliefs and habits when the people around you aren't necessarily joining in can feel a bit like you're the only person on an island. I call it feeling like you're zigging when the rest of the world is zagging.

If you do start feeling this, you can do some tapping and visualizations. Tap for the discomfort you're feeling. Visualize and tap for the experiences in relationships that you'd like to be having.

Also, because it's no coincidence that the word *action* is in the Law of Attraction, I also encourage you to seek out and get connected with fellow "ziggers." These are like-minded folks who are also on a journey of self-discovery and transformation. In this day and age it's easier than ever to connect to people. Maybe start a group in your area of folks who have read this book and are going to support each other through making changes. This Mastermind group can be as few as you and one other person, or as large as you want. The whole point is to surround yourself with folks so you can cheer each other on in your transformation process.

Or research more formal support groups or Mastermind groups on the Internet. Today, it's easier than ever to connect with like-minded people, and it will make this process much more enjoyable if you do.

You will likely even notice that as you begin finding your way in stepping into the happier "zigging you" that the people, places, and situations you are looking for and visualizing about begin showing up for you as if right on cue. Sometimes, even the current people in your life somehow change as you work on yourself. You'll understand this when it happens, and it's the coolest experience: seeing someone as familiar but also as if you're seeing them for the first time because your perspective has shifted.

And this brings me to...

## Act As If—and Other Things to Do in the Meantime

Remember the story of my miraculous weight loss-belief about my belt, and how for that entire day my actions were very different than my usual habits? For example, on that day, I was mindful of the foods I ate, I made a conscious choice to drink plenty of water, and overall I just acted as if I had lost weight and took steps to maintain it.

This is exactly what I mean by suggesting you "act as if." You plan, and take whatever actions you can now that you would take if your dream life was already your reality. Often people oppose this and write it off as impossible because of one reason or another, and if you caught those two clues I just used, then pat yourself on the back because you're on to me.

When we come up with "becauses" and "reasons" to not do something that is designed to support us in moving forward, it's a sign we're up against our limiting beliefs.

There simply *are* lots of things you can do, right now, with the current situations in your life that you would want to do if your dream life was your current experience. Just as I ate differently the whole day, eating and behaving as if I had already lost the weight, do what you can now with the resources you have—and then turn it up a notch and get creative.

If you want a new car, go to the dealership and take if for a test drive, call up a few places and price out the insurance for the new car so that you have the quotes ready, and make room in the garage. If you want to change careers, begin revamping your wardrobe (even just by window shopping) so that you'll be all set for when it's your reality and hang out at the places where people in your new field will hang out. If you want to move to your dream house, start clearing out the non-essential stuff you don't want to move, have a garage sale, begin packing the non-essential stuff, and store it until you're ready for the move. The list goes on and on. Have fun with your life transformation and "acting as if."

Other fun ideas also begin with the end in mind—as in, you imagine you're already experiencing what you want. One idea is to leave yourself a voice-mail message, as if you're talking to a friend, telling them all about your super cool news. In the message, describe what you want to manifest as if it has already happened.

If you've created a bit of a support group, have regular "success sessions" where you talk about your dream life and all its details as if it's your present reality. For example, talk about the trip are you planning for your upcoming two-month vacation and have the brochures you've been collecting with you as visuals, or talk about the color scheme you are having the builder use for the various rooms your lovely new dream house and again have visuals (perhaps the paint swatches), or talk about your business meetings and projections for the next six months, or what your new favorite clothing store is now that you've reached your ideal weight, or how you are doing with your new investments now that you've got a ton of disposable income for investing.

Another idea is to write yourself a letter as if it's five years from now and you're in your dream life. Describe what it is like basking in it and how it all came about by just dreaming about it until you began seeing it. I love this one because it's a bit like your future self coaching your now self. I often suggest putting the letter in a self-addressed, stamped envelope and giving it to a friend with instructions to mail it to you in about a month. These letters always seem to arrive just when needed to provide a real boost.

By "acting as if," you're creating new pathways and bringing your visualizations to reality.

Take note of and take action on the inspirations and "out of the blue" ideas that come to you, because they are the stepping stones path to the life of your dreams. Each time you notice these inspired thoughts or ideas and take an inspired step, the next step will be revealed. And before you know it, you will be stepping right into your dream life.

# Chapter 9

## Keep Your Eye on the Prize

The prize, in this game of life, is none other than all the happiness, inner peace, and love there is in the world. And it's all just waiting for you to invite it in to your life.

I think Marianne Williamson summed it up beautifully with:

*Our deepest fear is not that we are inadequate. Our deepest fear is that we are powerful beyond measure. It is our light, not our darkness that most frightens us. We ask ourselves, "Who am I to be brilliant, gorgeous, talented, fabulous?" Actually, who are you not to be? You are a child of God. Your playing small does not serve the world. There is nothing enlightened about shrinking so that other people won't feel insecure around you. We are all meant to shine, as children do. We were born to make manifest the glory of God that is within us. It's not just in some of us; it's in everyone. And as we let our own light shine, we unconsciously give other people permission to do the same. As we are liberated from our own fear, our presence automatically liberates others.*

My intention in writing this book was to offer you ideas, tools, inspiration, and proof that, no matter where you're starting from, be it a place that's dark and painful or a place where you're doing well and just want to take it to the next level, if you're ready to choose happiness for yourself, then you *can* get there from here.

Choose it for yourself and use the tools I've shared with you to step out of where you are and step into your Phenomenal Life.

September 2010 marked the ten-year anniversary of when I chose happiness for myself. And I've got to tell you, they've been the most interesting years of my life.

During the years before making that choice I was lonely and alone, living in a small, low-rent apartment with two cats as my only friends, tipping the scales at 210 pounds, working in a very stressful industry at a job that I felt was sucking the life out of me, taking part in a daily drinking habit believing it was the only way I could get by, and on the verge of suicide because my life was so dark, painful, and empty that I often wondered why I even bothered struggling *to* get by.

Had anyone told me then that my life could be phenomenal, and in fact, that within ten years I would be a mom to the most amazing boy, living in a house that I love just minutes from a beach where my son and I would play in the water on hot summer days, doing work I love, and making a difference in the lives of my clients, at a healthy weight, addiction-free, and connected with friends who are totally amazing, and all while taking inspired steps every day to create even more amazing experiences, to say I wouldn't have believed them is a an understatement of epic proportions.

But it's true. And if it can be done by me, it can be done by you!

Those first five or so years after I decided I could choose happiness, were spent searching for tools and trying them on in my life to find what worked. It was a bit like getting on an awesome roller coaster and taking that long, slow, first climb up to the top of the first hill. I knew something awesome would follow, but it was a bit of a slow-going ride in the beginning. But the five years since finding and incorporating the amazing tools I've shared with you in this book have just been an incredible ride. Today I'm flying along on the ride of my life using these tools every day while I'm dreaming up and stepping into even more "bliss door" experiences.

It is my pleasure to share this collection of tools and ideas with you to fast-track you up that first, giant hill of this wonderful ride called life.

I invite you to try them on, jump on, and enjoy the ride!!!

> *Life's journey is not to arrive at the grave safely in a well-preserved body, but rather to skid in sideways, totally worn out shouting "...holy sh\*t... what a ride!"*
>
> ~ Mavis Leyrer, at age 83

If you would like more information
about the services Mel provides through
Live In The Moment,
please visit www.liveinthemoment.ca

And while there,
be sure to sign up for
the "Friends Circle" to receive
your free mini-course
"Change Your Words to Change Your Life."

Made in the USA
Charleston, SC
30 April 2011